STANDARD ENCYCLOPEDIA OF
CARNIVAL GLASS

PRICE GUIDE

17TH EDITION

MIKE CARWILE

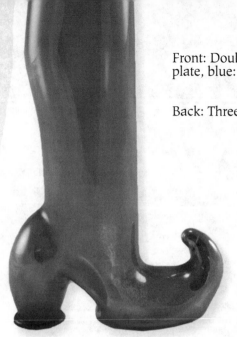

Front: Double Crossroads shakers, green: $125.00; amber: $140.00. Indiana Soldiers & Sailors plate, blue: $24,000.00. Three Fruits Intaglio bowl, marigold: $750.00.

Back: Three Fruits Intaglio bowl.

Cover design by Beth Summers
Book design by Lisa Henderson

A Personal Thank You
I first and most importantly want to thank God, and to thank my mother, Carolyn J. Carwile
(1927 – 2007), for introducing me to Him. It's been well worth it Mom.

Contact Mike Carwile @
email: mcarwile@jetbroadband.com
phone: 434-237-4247

Collector Books

P.O. Box 3009
Paducah, Kentucky 42002 – 3009

www.collectorbooks.com

Copyright © 2010 Mike Carwile

The current values in this book should be used only as a guide. They are not intended to set prices, which vary from one section of the country to another. Auction prices as well as dealer prices vary greatly and are affected by condition as well as demand. Neither the author nor the publisher assumes responsibility for any losses that might be incurred as a result of consulting this guide.

Searching for a Publisher?

We are always looking for people knowledgeable within their fields. If you feel that there is a real need for a book on your collectible subject and have a large comprehensive collection, contact Collector Books.

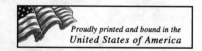
Proudly printed and bound in the United States of America

A 748.29

Writing a price guide for carnival glass is a difficult task because it not only must take into account patterns, colors, and shapes, but also the quality of the iridescence. Beginning collectors sometimes fail to understand that a price guide cannot easily reflect individual sales. At the same time, advanced collectors have complicated the mix by concocting new colors or shades of colors that affect prices. (See section The Basics of Carnival Glass Collecting in the front of this book for further guidance.)

In this guide you will notice that some prices have risen a great deal, some prices have remained nearly constant, and many prices have fallen substantially. (I've tried to cushion and slowly adjust some of these toward current market value to protect collectors, but not everyone will be satisfied I'm sure.) Most prices listed are based on research of auction sales (internet included), shop taggings, private sales where information was forthcoming, and a certain amount of speculation on items such as newly listed patterns which haven't established a current market value or one of a kind items which rarely come up for sale but certainly appreciate in value over the years.

Please remember no two pieces in the same color, pattern, shape, and size can be expected to bring identical prices, due to variation in iridescence, interest generated by a particular auction, and a host of other variables. (See section Grading Carnival Glass for additional pricing factors.) Please keep in mind that prices from older editions of this book cannot reflect today's market value and should be used only by well seasoned collectors. This is evident by a drastic decline in prices noted in this book (as well as the 11th edition) of most all glass coming from India (Jain, etc.) as the market was flooded with those pieces around 2005 – 2006, which caused this downward spiral in value.

This guide is only a general listing of, for the most part, average prices gathered in the year prior to publication. Use it only as a guide. Keep in mind that with internet sales at full speed you will see many items which were once considered rare reduced to scarce, and some items that were once listed as one of a kind dropped to rare, and so on. Sellers have seen the rare items sell over the years only to recognize that they have one of these on their shelf, thus putting another example into circulation and causing the price and desirability to drop.

Color Code

A — Amethyst or Purple	GO — Green Opalescent	PHO — Pastel Horehound
AB — Amberina	GW — Gold Wash	PK — Pink
ALS — Alaskan (Marigold Over Green)	HA — Honey Amber	PKA — Pink Afterglow
AM — Amber	HO — Horehound	PL — Pearl Opalescent
AMG — Amber Milk Glass	IB — Ice Blue	PM — Pastel Marigold
AO — Aqua Opalescent	IC — Iridized Custard	PO — Peach Opalescent
AP — Apricot	ICG — Iridized Chocolate Glass	R — Red
AQ — Aqua	IG — Ice Green	RA — Reverse Amberina
AS — Amethyst Swirl	IGO — Ice Green Opalescent	ReB — Renniger Blue
AT – O — Amethyst Opalescent	IL — Ice Lavender	RG — Russet Green (olive)
B — Blue	IM — Iridized Moonstone	RS — Red Slag
BA — Black Amethyst	IMG — Iridized Milk Glass	SA — Sapphire Blue
BLK — Black Glass	LG — Lime Green	SM — Smoke
BO — Blue Opalescent	LO — Lime Opalescent	SMG — Smoke Milk Glass
CeB — Celeste Blue	LV — Lavender	SO — Smokey Olive
CHP — Champagne	LVO — Lavender Opalescent	TG — Tangerine
CL — Clear	M — Marigold	TL — Teal
CLB — Colonial Blue	MMG — Marigold Milk Glass	V — Vaseline
CM — Clambroth	MUC — Mustard Custard	VI — Violet
CRAN — Cranberry Flash	NG — Nile Green	VO — Vaseline Opalescent
CRN — Cranberry	OB — Opaque Blue	W — White
CT — Citrene	OG — Olive Green	WO — White Opalescent
EB — Electric Blue	PaS — Pastel	WS — Wisteria
EmG — Emerald Green	PB — Powder Blue	Y — Yellow
G — Green	PeB — Persian Blue	ZB — Zircon Blue

Pattern Name	M	A	G	B	PO	AO	IB	IG	W	Red	Other
ABALONE											
Shade, very scarce									200		
ABSENTEE DRAGON (FENTON)											
Plate, rare	3800										
ABSENTEE FERN (FENTON)											
Pitcher, rare	3000										
*Variant of Butterfly and Fern – without Fern)											
ABSENTEE MINIATURE BLACKBERRY VARIANT											
Compote, small, stemmed	60	85	95	90							
*Variant of Miniature Blackberry with plain interior											
ACANTHUS (IMPERIAL)											
Banana Bowl	200										
Bowl, 8" – 9½"	55	200	100	275							140 AQ
Plate, 10"	165										350 SM
ACORN											
Vase, handled, rare	2800	3300	15000								7000 V
ACORN (FENTON)											
Bowl, 6¼" – 7½"	30	125	100	45	175	500			375	400	165 V
Plate, 8½", rare	2300	2200		2000					2500		2000 BA
ACORN (MILLERSBURG)											
Compote, rare	2000	2700	4000								6800 V
ACORN BURRS (NORTHWOOD)											
Bowl, flat, 5"	30	40	50								
Bowl, flat, 10"	90	250	175								
Covered Butter	225	300	800								
Covered Sugar	135	235	275								
Creamer or Spooner	95	115	225								
Punch Bowl and Base	1000	1600	2300	37000		39000	7900	15500	6000		
Punch Cup	45	75	85	100		1800	90	110	95		
Pitcher	550	575	800								
Tumbler	60	85	95						500		225 WS
Whimsey Vase, rare	3000	3600									
ACORN AND FILE											
Footed Compote, rare	1100	1400	1400								1500 V
ADAM'S RIB (DUGAN/DIAMOND)											
Bowl, large											150 MG
Candleholders, pair, pressed or blown	95							145			125 CeB
Compote								100			115 CeB
Covered Candy	90							135			110 CeB
Fan Vase	45							85			175 CeB
Juice Tumbler								95			75 CeB
Pitcher	160							400			425 CeB
Sugar, handled, open								90			
Tumbler	40							150			75 CeB
AFRICAN SHIELD (ENGLISH)											
Toothpick Holder (or Bud Holder)	175										
AGE HERALD (FENTON)											
Bowl, 9", scarce		1300									
Plate, 10", scarce		3300									
ALLAN'S RINGS											
Cracker Jar	75										
ALTERNATING DIMPLES											
Vase, enameled, eight sided	70										
AMAN (INDIA)											
Pitcher	365										
Tumbler	150										
AMARYLLIS (DUGAN)											
Compote, deep round	450			1000							
Compote, tricorner	300	400									
Plate Whimsey, very scarce	475	650							600		
AMERICAN (FOSTORIA)											
Rose Bowl, rare	400										
Toothpick Holder, rare	150										
Tumbler, rare	125		140								
Vase, very rare	300										
AMERICUS											
Tumbler, very scarce	75										
AMV											
Hand Vase	225										
ANCHOR HOCKING CRUET WHIMSEY											
Candlestick from cruet, very rare	300										
ANDEAN CHERRIES											
Tumbler, rare	200										
ANEMONE (NORTHWOOD)											
Pitcher	225										
Tumbler	25										
ANGELA											
Perfume	50										
ANGOORI											
Tumbler	175										
APOTHECARY JAR											
Small size	60										

Pattern Name	M	A	G	B	PO	AO	IB	IG	W	Red	Other
APPLE AND PEAR INTAGLIO (NORTHWOOD)											
Bowl, 5"	60										
Bowl, 10"	115										
APPLE BLOSSOM (DIAMOND)											
Bowl, 6" – 7½"	25	55	200	150	100				65		45 PK
Rose Bowl	125										
APPLE BLOSSOM (ENAMELED) (NORTHWOOD)											
Butter				200							
Creamer				100							
Pitcher				475							
Spooner				90							
Sugar				125							
Tumbler				90							
APPLE BLOSSOM TWIGS (DUGAN)											
Banana Bowl		350			300						
Bowl, 8" – 9"	40	175		200	375				125		400 SM
Plate, 8½"	200	325		350	400		2500		225		400 LV
Plate (smooth edge)		365			400						
APPLE PANELS (ENGLISH)											
Creamer	35										
Sugar (open)	35										
APPLE TREE (FENTON)											
Pitcher	300			1100					1200		
Tumbler	30			75					185		
Pitcher, vase whimsey, rare	7500			9000							1000 MMG
APRIL SHOWERS (FENTON)											
Vase	30	70	125	60					150	2400	1400 AT-O
A-Q											
Perfume, 4", rare		150									
ARABIAN BOOT											
Novelty Boot Miniature	75										
ARAMIS AND VARIANT (DUNBAR GLASS CORP)											
Hat Whimsey	75										
Pitcher, late (either shape)	60										
Tumbler, late (either shape)	10										
Vase Whimsey from pitcher	100										
ARCADIA BASKET											
Plate, 8"	50										
ARCADIA LACE (MCKEE)											
Rose Bowl	175										
Vase, 10", very scarce	225										
ARCHED FLEUR-DE-LIS (HIGBEE)											
Mug, rare	250										
ARCHED FLUTE (FENTON)											
Toothpick Holder		150 WS		125 CeB				125			100V
ARCHED PANELS											
Pitcher	185										
Tumbler	70										95 PB
ARCHES AND SAND											
Tumbler	200										
ARCS (IMPERIAL)											
Bowls, 8½"	30	60	50						175		35 CM
Compote	65	90									
ARGENTINA BLOSSOM											
Ink Well, very rare											3000 AM
ARGENTINA RIBBED BARREL											
Tumbler	125										
ARGENTINE HONEY POT											
Honey Jar w/lid	250										
ARMY HAT											
Hat Novelty	125										
ART DECO (GERMANY)											
Bowl, 4"	65										
Bowl, 8"	25										
Creamer	35										
Chop Plate, 12"	100										
ASTERS											
Bowl	60			100							
Compote	90										
Rose Bowl	200										
Vase	225										
ASTRAL											
Shade	55										
ATHENA											
Rose Bowl, 7"	140										
ATHENIA											
Toothpick Holder	450										
ATLANTIC CITY ELKS BELL											
1911 Atlantic City Bell, rare				2200							
AUCKLAND											
Vase, 7¼"	225										
AUGUST FLOWERS											
Shade	40										

Pattern Name	M	A	G	B	PO	AO	IB	IG	W	Red	Other
AURORA DAISIES											
Bowl, enameled											750 IM
AURORA PEARLS											
Bowl, two sizes, decorated		700		750						825	1350 IM
Bowl in Brides Basket											1750 IM
AURORA PRIMROSE SCROLL											
Bowl, enameled				850							
AURORA RUBINA VERDE											
Bowl, enameled and gilded											800
AUSTRAL											
Jug, 7¼"											125 AM
AUSTRALIAN DAISY (JAIN)											
Tumbler, very scarce	175										
AUSTRALIAN DAISY AND SHIELD (INDIA)											
Pitcher	325										
Tumbler	175										
AUSTRALIAN FILE BAND											
Exterior pattern only											
AUSTRALIAN HOLLY											
Bowl, footed, 7½"	275										
AUSTRALIAN KOOKABURRA											
Bowl, 9", lettered, very rare	1500										
AUTUMN ACORNS (FENTON)											
Bowl, 8½"	60	95	110	100						800	125 LG
Plate, 9" – 9½", scarce		1200	1550	1350							
AZTEC (MCKEE)											
Pitcher, rare	1300										
Tumbler, very scarce	650										
Creamer	250										250 CM
Sugar	250										250 CM
Rose Bowl											400 CM
AZTEC HEADDRESS											
Vase, 10", very scarce	325										
BABY BATHTUB (U. S. GLASS)											
Miniature Piece	225										
BABY'S BOUQUET											
Child's Plate, scarce	115										
BAKER'S ROSETTE											
Ornament	75	90									
BALL AND SWIRL											
Mug	120										
BALLARD-MERCED, CA (NORTHWOOD)											
Bowl	750										
Plate	1900										
BALLOONS (IMPERIAL)											
Cake Plate	85										110 SM
Compote	65										90 SM
Perfume Atomizer	60										90 SM
Vase, three sizes	75										100 SM
Vase, blank	65										
BAMBI											
Powder Jar w/lid	25										
BAMBOO BIRD											
Jar, complete	800										
BAMBOO SPIKE (CHINA)											
Tumbler	75										
BAND (DUGAN)											
Violet Hat	25	40			75						
BANDED DIAMONDS (CRYSTAL)											
Bowl, 5"	50	75									
Bowl, 9"	100	125									
Flower Set, two pieces	150	195									
Pitcher, very scarce	900	1250									
Tumbler, very scarce	250	400									
BANDED DIAMONDS AND BARS											
Decanter, complete	200										
Plate	200										
Tumbler, 2¼"	475										
Tumbler, 4"	450										
BANDED DIAMOND AND FAN (ENGLISH)											
Compote, 6"	100										
Toothpick Holder	80										
BANDED DRAPE (FENTON)											
Pitcher	200		500	400					750		
Tumbler	40		75	50					95		
BANDED FLUTE											
Compote, 4½", scarce	60										
BANDED GRAPE (FENTON)											
Mini Creamer	75										
BANDED GRAPE AND LEAF (JAIN)											
Pitcher, rare	650										
Tumbler, rare	100										

Pattern Name	M	A	G	B	PO	AO	IB	IG	W	Red	Other
BANDED KNIFE AND FORK											
Shot Glass	75										
BANDED LAUREL WREATH											
Juice Tumbler, footed	25										
BANDED MOON AND STARS (JAIN)											
Tumbler, rare	225										
BANDED MOON AND STARS VARIANT (JAIN)											
Tumbler, rare	275										
BANDED NECK											
Vase	50										
BANDED PANELS (CRYSTAL)											
Open Sugar	45	60									
BANDED PORTLAND (U.S. GLASS)											
Puff Jar	125										
Salt Shaker	90										
Toothpick	150										
Tumbler	150										
BANDED RIB											
Pitcher	125										
Tumbler, two sizes	40										
BANDED RIB NECK VASE (CZECH)											
Vase w/black band	75										
BANDED ROSE											
Vase, small	175										
BAND OF ROSES											
Pitcher	250										
Tumbler	150										
Tray	75										
Tumble-up, two pieces	200										
BAND OF STARS											
Decanter	175										
Wine, stemmed	35										
BARBELLA (NORTHWOOD)											
Bowl	50										70 V
Plate	70										85 TL
Tumbler											225 V
BARBER BOTTLE (CAMBRIDGE)											
Complete	575	750	750								
BARBER BOTTLE (CZECH)											
Cordial Bottle	60										
Stemmed Cordial	40										
Tray	50										
BAROQUE											
Tumbler, very rare	500										
BARREL											
Tumbler, scarce											150 V
BASKET OF ROSES (NORTHWOOD)											
Bonbon, scarce	325	550		480							300 V
Stippled, add 25%											
BASKETWEAVE (NORTHWOOD)											
Compote	60	75	95	120							
BASKETWEAVE AND CABLE (WESTMORELAND)											
Creamer w/lid	50	75	100						175		
Sugar w/lid	50	75	100						175		
Syrup Whimsey	180										
BASKETWEAVE/VINTAGE VARIATION											
See Vintage (Northwood)											
BAVARIAN BERRY											
Enameled Pitcher	240										
BEADED ACANTHUS (IMPERIAL)											
Milk Pitcher	300		375								175 SM
BEADED BAND AND OCTAGON											
Kerosene Lamp	250										
BEADED BASKET (DUGAN)											
Basket, flared	50	325	375	350					225		350 AQ
Basket, straight sided, rare	85	350							325		450 AQ
BEADED BLOCK											
Milk Pitcher											75 CM
BEADED BULL'S EYE (IMPERIAL)											
Vase, 8" – 14"	65	235	200								240 AM
Vase, squat, 5½" – 7½"	85	300	185								
Vase, mold proof, scarce	125										
BEADED CABLE (NORTHWOOD)											
Candy Dish	50	70	80	185		200	135	160	200		8000 IC
Rose Bowl	75	125	250	295	10000	350	400	750	275		375 IL
(Ribbed interior, add 25%)											
BEADED DAISY PANELS (GERMAN)											
Compote, scarce	125										
BEADED FLORAL BAND											
Tumbler	25										
BEADED HEARTS (NORTHWOOD)											
Bowl	50	85	90								
BEADED LOOP (OREGON)											
Vase Whimsey	100										

Pattern Name	M	A	G	B	PO	AO	IB	IG	W	Red	Other
BEADED MIRRORS (JAIN)											
Tumbler, rare	200										
BEADED MIRRORS VARIANT (JAIN)											
Tumbler, rare	250										
BEADED MIRRORS WITH ETCHED FLOWERS (JAIN)											
Tumbler	150										
BEADED OVAL AND FAN											
Shaker, rare											125 V
BEADED PANELS (DUGAN)											
Compote	60	225		350	95						
BEADED PANELS (IMPERIAL)											
Bowl, 5"	25										
Bowl 8"	45										
Powder Jar w/lid	50										
BEADED PANELS AND GRAPES (JAIN)											
Tumbler	275										
BEADED SHELL (DUGAN)											
Bowl, footed, 5"	35	40									
Bowl, footed, 9"	75	95									
Covered Butter	130	150									
Covered Sugar	90	110									
Creamer or Spooner	75	90									
Mug	145	80		175							175 LV
Mug Whimsey		450							700		
Pitcher	500	650									
Tumbler	60	70		180							
BEADED SPEARS (JAIN)											
Pitcher, rare	490	560									
Tumbler, rare	190	200									
BEADED SPEARS VARIANTS (JAIN)											
Tumbler	225			300							
BEADED STAR MEDALLION											
Shade, either	75										
BEADED STARS (FENTON)											
Banana Boat	25										
Bowl	20										
Plate, 9"	65										
Rose Bowl	50										
BEADED SWAG MEDALLION											
Vase, 5½", scarce	350										
BEADED SWIRL (ENGLISH)											
Compote	50			60							
Covered Butter	70			85							
Milk Pitcher	75			90							
Sugar	50			55							
BEADED TEARDROPS (FOSTORIA)											
Vase, 6"	150										
BEADS (NORTHWOOD)											
Bowl, 8½"	45	60	70								
BEADS AND BARS (U.S. GLASS)											
Rose Bowl, rare	350										300 CM
Spooner, rare	125										
BEARDED BERRY (FENTON)											
Exterior pattern only											
BEAUTY BUD VASE (DIAMOND)											
Tall Vase, no twigs	20	75									
BEE											
Ornament	275										
BEETLE ASHTRAY (ARGENTINA)											
One size, rare	650			500							850 AM
BELLAIRE SOUVENIR (IMPERIAL)											
Bowl, scarce	125										
BELL FLOWER (FUCHSIA)											
Compote, handled, rare	2200			2000							
BELLFLOWER VASE											
Vase, very rare				1200							
BELLS AND BEADS (DUGAN)											
Bowl, 7½"	45	90	115	120	90						
Compote	70	75									
Gravy Boat, handled	55	70			140						
Hat shape	40	60									
Nappy	60	95			100						
Plate, 8"		170									
BELTED RIB											
Vase, 8"	95										
BENZER											
Car Vase	90								125		
BERNHEIMER (MILLERSBURG)											
Bowl, 8¾", scarce				2500							
BERRY LEAF											
Mustard w/lid	700										
BERRY BASKET											
One size	50										
Matching Shakers, pair	75										

Pattern Name	M	A	G	B	PO	AO	IB	IG	W	Red	Other
BERTHA (BROCKWITZ)											
Bowls	45 – 95										
Butter, covered	200										
Creamer	35										
Sugar, open	30										
BIG BASKETWEAVE (DUGAN)											
Basket, small	25	60									
Basket, large	75	145									
Vase, squat, 4" – 7"	125	200			300				150		250 HO
*(4" is also base for Persian Garden Punch Bowl)											
Vase, 8" – 14"	75	200		300	425		600		100		450 LV
BIG CHIEF											
One Shape		95									
BIG FISH (MILLERSBURG)											
Bowl, 8½"	600	625	750								6250 V
Bowl, tricornered	5000	9000	13000								2000 V
Bowl, square, rare	1000	1800	2000								5800 V
Bowl, square (fish turned left, very rare)			2800								
Banana Bowl, rare		1900	1900								
Rose Bowl, very rare		10000									11000 V
BIG THISTLE (MILLERSBURG)											
Punch Bowl and Base, very rare		15000									
BIRD AND STRAWBERRY											
Tumbler, very scarce	150										
BIRD EPERGNE (CZECH)											
Epergne	150										
BIRD GALAXY											
Vase, 10¼", very rare			4200						3800		4000 IMG
BIRD-IN-THE-BUSH (GERMANY)											
Tumbler	250										
BIRD OF PARADISE (NORTHWOOD)											
Bowl, advertising		400									
Plate, advertising		450									
BIRD SALT DIP											
Novelty Salt Dip	75										
BIRDS AND CHERRIES (FENTON)											
Bonbon	40	125	80	65							
Bowl, 9½", rare	200	325		375							
Bowl, 10", ice cream shape, rare				1800							
Compote	45	60	85	60							
Plate, 10", rare	2000	16000		3000							
BIRD WITH GRAPES (COCKATOO)											
Wall Vase	125										
BISHOP'S MITRE (FINLAND)											
Vase 8"	150			200							
BLACK BAND (CZECH)											
Vase, 2 shapes, 4" – 4½"	75										
BLACKBERRY (AKA: BLACKBERRY OPEN EDGE BASKET) (FENTON)											
Hat Shape	35	150	165	50					135	400	85 LG
Plate, rare	1350			1800							
Spittoon Whimsey, rare	3200			3600							
Vase Whimsey, rare	925			1700					800	3000	
BLACKBERRY (NORTHWOOD)											
Compote, either exterior pattern	85	100	150	325					150		
BLACKBERRY BANDED (FENTON)											
Hat Shape	35	75	55	45	135				200		125 IM
BLACKBERRY BARK											
Vase, rare		12000									
BLACKBERRY BLOCK (FENTON)											
Pitcher	400	1250	1400	1250							6500 V
Tumbler	65	80	95	75							350 V
BLACKBERRY BRAMBLE (FENTON)											
Compote	40	50	70	55							
BLACKBERRY/DAISY AND PLUME (NORTHWOOD)											
Candy Dish, three footed, Berry interior	90	200	165	1500			750	900	500		900 LG
Rose Bowl, three footed, Berry interior	100	185	175	900		9000	1300	1150	550		1000 AM
BLACKBERRY INTAGLIO											
Plate, 6"	165										
BLACKBERRY RAYS (NORTHWOOD)											
Compote	425	450	500								
BLACKBERRY SPRAY (FENTON)											
Bonbon	35	45	50	45							400 AB
Compote	40	50	55	50							
Hat Shape	45	100	200	40		800				400	135 AQ
Absentee Variant, J.I.P									55	45	
BLACKBERRY SPRAY VARIANT (FENTON)											
Hat Shape	65									450	125 AQ
BLACKBERRY WREATH AND VARIANTS (MILLERSBURG)											
Bowl, 5½"	175	125	95								125 CM
Bowl, sauce, decorated, rare	500										

Pattern Name	M	A	G	B	PO	AO	IB	IG	W	Red	Other
Bowl, 7" – 9"	75	125	110	1300							
Bowl, 10"	95	300	325	1650							
Plate, 6", rare	1400	1200	2800								
Plate, 8", rare			4200								
Plate, 10", very rare	7000	7500									
Spittoon Whimsey, rare			8000								
BLACK BOTTOM (FENTON)											
Candy w/lid, either size	50										
Candy w/lid, decorated,											
very scarce	90										
BLAZING CORNUCOPIA											
(U.S. GLASS)											
Spooner, very scarce	150										
BLOCK BAND DIAMOND											
(U.S. GLASS)											
Berry Bowl, small	75										
Berry Bowl, large	125										
Butter	300										
Creamer	90										
Spooner	90										
Sugar w/lid	115										
Syrup, decorated, rare	250										
Tumbler	150										
*All pieces scarce to rare and have											
enameled decoration											
BLOCKS AND ARCHES (CRYSTAL)											
Creamer	40										
Pitcher, rare	100	140									
Tumbler, rare	75	90									
BLOSSOM (JENKINS)											
Covered Jar	100										
BLOSSOM AND SHELL											
(NORTHWOOD)											
Bowl, 9"	50	65	70								90 ALS
BLOSSOM AND SPEARS											
Plate, 8"	50										
BLOSSOMS AND BAND											
Bowl, 5"	20	30									
Bowl, 10"	30	40									
Wall Vase, complete	45										
BLOSSOMTIME (NORTHWOOD)											
Compote	275	325	425								
BLOWN CANDLESTICKS											
One Size, pair	90										
BLUEBELL BAND AND RIBS											
(ARGENTINA)											
Pitcher, very scarce				500							
BLUEBERRY (FENTON)											
Pitcher, scarce	500			2000							
Tumbler, scarce	45		150	100						200	
BLUE RING (CZECH)											
Decanter	200										
Shot Glass, each	35										
BLUM DEPARTMENT STORE											
Tumbler, rare	300										
BOGGY BAYOU (FENTON)											
Vase, 6" – 11"	40	125	150	135							800 LGO
Vase, 12" – 15"	60	145	160	150							
BOND (BROCKWITZ)											
Vase	145			225							
BOOKER											
Cider Pitcher	500										
Mug	100										
BOOT											
One shape	150										
BO PEEP (WESTMORELAND)											
ABC Plate, scarce	550										
Mug, scarce	160										
BORDER PLANTS (DUGAN)											
Bowl, flat, 8½"		125			180						
Bowl, footed, 8½"	175	475			250						
Handgrip Plate	350	495			350						
Rose Bowl, scarce		700			525						
BOSTON											
Vase		300									
BOTTLE ASHTRAY											
Whimsey, one shape	100										
BOUQUET (FENTON)											
Pitcher	285			485							
Tumbler	30			100							
BOUQUET TOOTHPICK HOLDER											
One size	75										
BOUTONNIERE (MILLERSBURG)											
Compote	100	135	150								
BOW AND KNOT											
Perfume	45										

Pattern Name	M	A	G	B	PO	AO	IB	IG	W	Red	Other
BOXED STAR											
One Shape, rare										110	
BOY AND LAMP POST											
Candleholder, rare	225										
BRAND FURNITURE (FENTON)											
Open Edge Basket, advertising	90										
BRAZIERS CANDIES (FENTON)											
Bowl		675									
Plate, handgrip		1000									
BREAKFAST SET (INDIANA)											
Creamer or Sugar, each	50										
BRIAR PATCH											
Hat shape	40	50									
BRIDE'S BOUQUET (JAIN)											
Tumbler, scarce	250										
BRIDE'S VASE											
Vase in Metal Stand	25			30							25 CL
BRIDE'S WALL VASE											
Vase in Holder	50										75 SM
BRIDLE ROSETTE											
One shape	85										
BRILLIANT MEDALLIONS (INWALD)											
Bowl, 5"	95										
BRITT (KARHULA)											
Pitcher, very rare				5000							
Tumbler, very rare	400			600							
BROCADED ACORNS (FOSTORIA)											
Bowl w/handle							115				
Cake Tray, center handle							200				
Candleholder, each							85				
Compote							165				65 LV
Covered Box							185				
Ice Bucket							255				325 LV
Pitcher, rare							1700				
Tray							135				
Tumbler							65				
Vase							200				
BROCADED BASE											
Vase		65									
BROCADED DAFFODILS (FOSTORIA)											
Bonbon							100	90			
Cake Plate, handled							125	85			
Cake Tray							150				
Flower Set							225				
Vase							200				
BROCADED DAISES (FOSTORIA)											
Bonbon								70			
Bowl								100			
Tray								210			
Vase								275			
Wine Goblet								200			
BROCADED PALMS (FOSTORIA)											
Bonbon								55			
Bread Tray								185			
Cake Plate								150			
Covered Box								225			
Dome Bowl								85			
Footed Center Bowl								225			
Ice Bucket								250			
Planter w/frog								500			
Rose Bowl								175			
Vase								225			
BROCADED POPPIES (FOSTORIA)											
Bonbon								75			
Bowl								100			
Cake Tray								150			125 PK
Vase								285			
BROCADED ROSES (FOSTORIA)											
Bonbon								75			
Cake Plate w/center handle								200			
Covered Box								185			
Dome Bowl								100			
Ice Bucket								295			
Large Footed Bowl								210			
Rose Bowl								145			
Tray								175			
Wine Goblet								200			
Vase								300			
BROCADED SUMMER GARDENS											
Bonbon									75		
Cake Plate w/center handle									85		
Compote									100		
Covered Box									100		
Covered Sectional Dish									125		
Ice Bucket									145		

Pattern Name	M	A	G	B	PO	AO	IB	IG	W	Red	Other
Large Footed Bowl									75		
Plate									65		
Rose Bowl									80		
Sweetmeat w/lid									125		
Tumbler									125		
Tray									75		
Vase									50		
Wine Goblet									40		
BROCKWITZ HENS											
Hen w/lid, small	225										
Hen w/lid, large	300										
BROCKWITZ STAR											
Vase, scarce	200										
BROEKER'S FLOUR (NORTHWOOD)											
Plate, advertising		3000									
BROKEN ARCHES (IMPERIAL)											
Bowl, 8½" – 10"	45	50	75								
Punch Bowl and Base, round top	400	1100									
Punch Cup	20	45									
Punch Bowl and Base, ruffled top and ringed interior pattern, rare		2000									
BROKEN CHAIN AKA: S-BAND (CRYSTAL)											
Bowl	90	150									
BROKEN BRANCH (FOSTORIA)											
Vase	165										
BROKEN RING SHAKER											
Individual Shaker	50										
BROOKLYN											
Bottle w/stopper	75	95									
BROOKLYN BRIDGE (DIAMOND)											
Bowl, scarce	325										
BROOKLYN BRIDGE UNLETTERED											
Bowl, unlettered, rare	4700										
BUBBLE BERRY											
Shade											75 CRAN
BUBBLES											
Lamp Chimney											50 HO
BUBBLE WAVES											
Compote, rare					150						
BUCKINGHAM (U.S. GLASS)											
Open Sugar	165										
BUD VASE WHIMSEY (FENTON)											
Vase, two or four sides up	50			100							125 CeB
BUDDHA											
6" size, sitting, rare	2000			2300					2000		
10" size, sitting, rare			2500								
BUDDHA VARIANT											
Large size, reclining position, rare	2200										
BULLDOG											
Paperweight	200										
BULLDOG WITH BOW											
Novelty	1250										
BULL RUSH AND ORCHIDS											
Bowl, 8" – 9"	90										
Plate	250										
BULL'S EYE (U.S. GLASS)											
Oil Lamp	210										
BULL'S EYE AND BEADS (FENTON)											
Vase, 14" – 18"	125			150							
BULL'S EYE AND DIAMONDS											
Mug	150										
BULL'S EYE AND LEAVES (NORTHWOOD)											
Bowl, 8½"	40	55	50								
BULL'S EYE AND LOOP (MILLERSBURG)											
Vase, 7" – 11", rare	600	500	400								
BULL'S EYE AND SPEARHEAD											
Wine	90										
BUNNY											
Bank	30										
BUSHEL BASKET (NORTHWOOD)											
One shape, footed	100	90	300	125		375	350	275	200		350 HO
BUSHEL BASKET VARIANT (NORTHWOOD)											
Basket, smooth handle, very scarce	450	350	600								
BUTTERFLIES (FENTON)											
Bonbon	60	70	75	65							
Bonbon, advertising (Horlacher)		125									
Card Tray	55			60							
BUTTERFLY (JEANNETTE)											
Pin Tray	10										15 TL
Party Set (complete in box)	75										95 TL
BUTTERFLY (FENTON)											
Ornament, rare	1800	2000	2200	2400			1600	1700	1200		1350 AQ

12

Pattern Name	M	A	G	B	PO	AO	IB	IG	W	Red	Other
BUTTERFLY (NORTHWOOD)											
Bonbon, regular	50	75	125	325							
Bonbon, threaded exterior	700	400	1100	625			3250				
BUTTERFLY (U.S. GLASS)											
Tumbler, very rare	6500		10000								
BUTTERFLY AND BERRY (FENTON)											
Bowl, footed, 5"	25	85	110	125					95	1000	
Bowl, footed, 10"	85	225	200	135					725		
Bowl, 5" tricorner whimsey, very rare				3500							
Bowl Whimsey (fernery)	600	500		800							
Centerpiece Bowl, rare				1400							
Covered Butter	130	240	300	225							
Creamer or Spooner	40	150	200	85							
Covered Sugar	70	160	200	150							
Hatpin Holder, scarce	1900			2100							
Hatpin Holder Whimsey, rare	2300										
Nut Bowl Whimsey		700									
Plate, 6", footed, very rare	1000										
Plate, footed, whimsey				1500							
Pitcher	300	500	750	500					1500		
Tumbler	30	65	125	85							325 V
Spittoon Whimsey, two types		3000		3000							
Vase, 6½" – 9"	35	85	300	100					150	850	500 AQ
BUTTERFLY AND CORN											
Vase, very rare	6500	15000	16000								9000 V
BUTTERFLY AND FERN (FENTON)											
Pitcher	325	400	650	425							
Tumbler	45	55	85	65							
Variant Pitcher (no ferns), rare	3000										
BUTTERFLY AND FLANNEL FLOWER											
Compote, ruffled	150										
Compote, round	100										
BUTTERFLY AND PLUME											
Tumbler			125								
BUTTERFLY AND SINGLE FLOWER											
Oil Lamp											425
BUTTERFLY AND TULIP (DUGAN)											
Bowl, footed, 10½", scarce	350	2500			13500						
Bowl, whimsey, rare	600	2700									
BUTTERFLY BOWER (CRYSTAL)											
Bowl, 9"	115	150									
Cake Plate, stemmed		200									
Compote	225	325									
BUTTERFLY BUSH (CRYSTAL)											
Cake Plate, 10", rare	450										
Compote, large	220	300									
BUTTERFLY BUSH AND CHRISTMAS BELLS											
Compote	220	245									
BUTTERFLY BUSH AND FLANNEL FLOWER (CRYSTAL)											
Compote, ruffled	175										
BUTTERFLY BUSH AND WARATAH (CRYSTAL)											
Compote	200	400									
BUTTERFLY LAMP											
Oil Lamp	1500										
BUTTERMILK GOBLET (FENTON)											
Goblet	50	75	85							125	
BUTTONS AND DAISY (IMPERIAL)											
Hat (old only)											70 CM
Slipper (old only)											80 CM
BUTTONS AND STARS (NORWAY)											
Sugar Basket	70										
BUTTRESS (U.S. GLASS)											
Pitcher, rare	450										
Tumbler, rare	250										
BUZZ SAW											
Shade	40										
BUZZ SAW (CAMBRIDGE)											
Cruet, 4", scarce			575								
Cruet, 4", with metal tag lettered:			1000								
B.P.O.E. #1, rare	425		400								
Cruet, 6", scarce											
BUZZ SAW (EUROPEAN)											
Pitcher	100										
BUZZ SAW AND FILE											
Goblet	145										
Pitcher	325										
Tumbler, juice	125										
Tumbler, lemonade	150										
BUZZ SAW AND FILE FRAMED											
Candy w/lid	95										
Bowl, 5½"	75										
BUZZ SAW SHADE											
Lamp Shade, scarce	75										

Pattern Name	M	A	G	B	PO	AO	IB	IG	W	Red	Other
CACTUS (MILLERSBURG)											
Exterior only											
CALCUTTA DIAMONDS (INDIA)											
Pitcher	325										
Tumbler	125										
CALCUTTA ROSE (INDIA)											
Tumbler	135										
CAMBRIDGE #2351											
Bowl, 9", rare			350								
Punch Bowl w/base, very rare	1500										
Punch Cup, scarce		65	65								
Vase, 4", rare	500										
CAMBRIDGE #2660/108											
*See Near Cut (Cambridge)											
CAMBRIDGE #2760 (VARIANT OF SUNK DAISY)											
Shakers, each	100										
CAMBRIDGE COLONIAL #2750											
Cruet, rare	450										
CAMBRIDGE HOBSTAR (CAMBRIDGE)											
Napkin Ring	165										
CAMEO (FENTON)											
Vase, 11" – 17", scarce											250 CeB
CAMEO MEDALLION BASKET (WESTMORELAND)											
Basket, three sizes	35 – 75										
CAMEO PENDANT											
Cameo		250									
CAMIELLA LOOP											
Vase, 5¾"	150										
CAMPBELL BEASLEY (MILLERSBURG)											
Plate, advertising, handgrip		1400									
CANADA DRY											
Bottle, two sizes	25								45		
Tumbler Whimsey, cut from bottle	45										
*Double price for unopened bottle with all labels.											
CANARY TREE (JAIN)											
Tumbler	235										
CAN-CAN											
Candy Tray	155										
CANDLE DRIP VASE											
Vase, 5", rare	300										
CANDLE LAMP (FOSTORIA)											
One size	110										
CANDLE VASE											
One size	55										
CANDLE VASE VARIANT (DUGAN)											
Vase, 12"											75 CeB
CANE (EUROPEAN)											
Tankard	170										
CANE AND DAISY CUT											
Basket, handled, rare	220										250 SM
Vase	150										
CANE AND PANELS											
Tumbler	200										
Tumble-up	350										
CANE AND SCROLL (SEA THISTLE) (ENGLISH)											
Creamer or Sugar	45										
Rose Bowl	125			75							
CANE AND WEDGE (FINLAND)											
Vase, 4⅞"											250 AM
CANE OPEN EDGE BASKET (IMPERIAL)											
Basket, squat, very rare											500 MMG
CANE PANELS											
Vase	85										
CANNONBALL VARIANT											
Pitcher	240			285					400		
Tumbler	40			50					75		
CANOE (U.S. GLASS)											
One size	150										
CAPITOL (WESTMORELAND)											
Bowl, footed, small		70		70							
Mug, small	140										
CAPTIVE ROSE (FENTON)											
Bonbon	45	80	125	105							
Bowl, 8½" – 10"	50	110	70	80							250 BA
Compote	70	80	100	95					100		125 PB
Plate, 9"	500	850	950	875							
CARLTEC											
Pickle or Relish Dish	125										

Pattern Name	M	A	G	B	PO	AO	IB	IG	W	Red	Other
CARNATION (NEW MARTINSVILLE)											
Punch Cup	50										
CARNATION WREATH											
Bowl, 9½", scarce	125										
CARNIVAL BEADS											
Various strands	30+										
CARNIVAL BUTTONS											
Buttons, various sizes and designs		15 – 40		20 – 50							
CARNIVAL CRUETS											
Cruets, various designs	50 – 75										
CARNIVAL BELL											
One size	425										
CARNIVAL CRUETS											
Cruets, various designs	50 – 75										
CAROLINA DOGWOOD (WESTMORELAND)											
Bowl, 8½"	80	110				450					150 MMG
Plate, rare											300 BO
CAROLINE (DUGAN)											
Bowl, 7" – 10"	70	275			100						
Banana Bowl					125						
Basket, scarce					250						600 LVO
CARRIE (ANCHOR-HOCKING)											
One size	60										
CARTWHEEL, #411 (HEISEY)											
Bonbon	60										
Compote	50										
Goblet	75										
CAR VASE											
Automobile Vase	45										
CASTLE											
Shade	50										
CAT BANK											
Novelty Bank/Beverage Container	125										
CAT FACE (ARGENTINA)											
Ashtray Novelty	250										
CATHEDRAL ARCHES											
Compote, large, tall, rare				700							
Punch Bowl, one piece	425										
CATHEDRAL WINDOWS (INDIA)											
Pitcher	325										
Tumbler	135										
CB VASE (INDIA)											
Vase, 6"	275										
CB VASE VARIANT (INDIA)											
Vase	275										
CELEBRATION (JAIN)											
Tumbler	225										
CELESTIAL BAND											
Tumbler, 3¼", very scarce	150										
CENTRAL SHOE STORE (FENTON)											
Bowl, 6" – 7"		1000									
Plate, scarce		2500									
Plate, handgrip		1200									
CHAIN AND STAR (FOSTORIA)											
Covered Butter, rare	1500										
Creamer or Sugar	175										
Tumbler, rare	900										
CHANNELED FLUTE (NORTHWOOD)											
Vase, 10" – 16"	65	90	100								150 ALS
CHARIOT											
Compote, large	100										
Creamer, stemmed/opened	70										
Sugar	65										
CHARLIE (SWEDEN)											
Bowl	100			200							
Rose Bowl	250			375							
CHARLOTTE (BROCKWITZ)											
Compote, large	325			450							
CHARLOTTE'S WEB											
Mirror	275										200 PK
CHATELAINE (IMPERIAL)											
Pitcher, very scarce		3000									
Tumbler, very scarce		300									
CHATHAM (U.S. GLASS)											
Candlesticks, pair	90										
Compote	75										
CHECKERBOARD (WESTMORELAND)											
Cruet, rare											750 CM
Goblet, rare	350	250									
Punch Cup, scarce	80										
Pitcher, rare		3000									
Tumbler, rare	675	400									
Wine, rare	300										
Vase, scarce		2400									

Pattern Name	M	A	G	B	PO	AO	IB	IG	W	Red	Other
CHECKERBOARD BOUQUET											
Plate, 8"	80										
CHECKERBOARD PANELS (ENGLISH)											
Bowl	70										
CHECKERBOARD PIPE HOLDER ASHTRAY											
Ashtray with Pipe Holder	225										
CHECKERS											
Ashtray	40										
Bowl, 4"	25										
Bowl, 9"	35										
Butter, 2 sizes	200										
Plate, 7"	75										
Rose Bowl	85										
CHEROKEE											
Tumbler				65							
CHERRIES AND DAISES (FENTON)											
Banana Boat	800			1000							
CHERRIES AND LITTLE FLOWERS (FENTON)											
Pitcher	175	265		325							
Tumbler	25	35		40							
CHERRY (DUGAN)											
Banana Bowl		300			250						
Bowl, flat, 5" – 7"	30	60			50				125		
Bowl, flat, 8" – 10"	100	300			250				525		
Bowl, footed, 8½"	75	375		600	225						
Bowl Proof Whimsey				500							
Chop Plate, 11", very rare		4000									
Plate, 6"		300			250						
CHERRY (FENTON)											
See Mikado Compote											
CHERRY (MILLERSBURG)											
(AKA: Hanging Cherries)											
Banana Compote, rare		4000									
Bowl, 5½"	75	125	90	1800							
Bowl, 7" "	100	125	165	2600							
Bowl, 9", scarce	150	250	250								
Bowl, 10"	175	300	340	2800							375 AQ
Bowl, 5", Hobnail exterior, rare			1000	1800							
Bowl, 9", Hobnail exterior, rare	1650	2500		3350							
Bowl, 9" – 10", plain back, rare		475									
Compote, large, rare	1250	2800	1650	4500							5000 V
Compote Whimsey, either shape, rare		5000									
Covered Butter	250	375	450								
Covered Sugar	170	300	325								
Creamer	75	175	250								275 TL
Milk Pitcher, rare	1600	900	1100	7000							
Pitcher, very scarce	1800	1400	2000	8000							
Tumbler, two variations	135	175	200								
Tumbler, goofus, experimental			500								
Spooner	100	175	200								
Plate, 6", rare	3400										
Plate, 7½", rare	825	3000	4300								
Plate, 10", rare	2500	3500	3700								
Powder Jar, very rare	4600		3800								5000 MMG
CHERRY AND CABLE (NORTHWOOD)											
Bowl, 5", scarce	75										
Bowl, 9", scarce	110										
Butter, scarce	400										
Pitcher, scarce	1200										
Tumbler, scarce	150										
Sugar, Creamer, Spooner, each, scarce	175			350							
CHERRY AND CABLE INTAGLIO (NORTHWOOD)											
Bowl, 5"	50										
Bowl, 10"	75										
CHERRY BLOSSOMS											
Pitcher				150							
Tumbler				40							
CHERRY CHAIN (FENTON)											
Bonbon	50	60	65	60							
Bowl, small, 4½" – 5"	25	60	75	50							45 CM
Bowl, 9" – 10"	70	350	300	85					100	6500	150 V
Plate, 6" "	115	900	1350	175					250		1700 EmG
Chop Plate, rare	2100								1300		
CHERRY CHAIN VARIANT (FENTON)											
Bowl, 7" – 9"	55	135	300	135					7000		
Plate, 9½"	225	600	850	225							
CHERRY CIRCLES (FENTON)											
Bonbon	45	125	200	95						4000	225 PB
CHERRY SMASH (CHERRYBERRY) (U.S. GLASS)											
Bowl, 8"	55										
Butter	160										
Compote, 3¾", scarce	75										

Pattern Name	M	A	G	B	PO	AO	IB	IG	W	Red	Other
Pitcher, very scarce	225										
Tumbler	150										
CHERRY VARIANT (DUGAN)											
Bowl, footed, rare		400									
CHERRY VARIANT (MILLERSBURG)											
Plate, 11", rare		7000									
Bowl, 10", very scarce		900	1100								
CHERUB											
Lamp, rare											150 CL
CHERUBS											
Mini Toothpick Holder	200										
CHESTERFIELD (IMPERIAL)											
Candy w/lid, tall	65									300	90 SM
Champagne, 5½"	35									175	50 SM
Candlesticks, pair	60										105 SM
Compote, 6½"	35										40 CM
Compote, petal crimped top	85										
Compote, 11½"	75								95	400	125 SM
Creamer or Sugar	45									175	
Lemonade Pitcher	150								300	8000	
Lemonade Tumbler	35								145	1500	
Punch Bowl and Base	500										
Punch Cup	50										
Rose Bowl, collar base	45										60 SM
Lemonade Mug, handled	50								110		40 CM
Salt, open, stemmed	65										
Sherbet	25									80	50 TL
Table Salt	85										60 CM
Toothpick, handled	225										
Whimsey from Compote, 6¾", rare	200										
(Add 25% for Iron Cross)											
CHEVRONS											
Vase, very scarce	325										
CHILD'S PUNCH CUP											
Child's punch set cup	65										
CHIPPENDALE KRY-STOL (JEFFERSON)											
Bonbon, small, stemmed	35										
Bonbon, large, stemmed	60										
CHIPPENDALE SOUVENIR											
Creamer or Sugar	65	85									
CHRIST CANDLESTICK											
Candleholder, rare	700										
CHRISTMAS COMPOTE (DUGAN)											
Large Compote, scarce	5700	4500									
CHRYSANTHEMUM (FENTON)											
Bowl, flat, 9"	65	95	200	100					500	5500	250 TL
Bowl, footed, 10"	50	80	225	225						3500	325 V
Plate, very rare	2000										
CHRYSANTHEMUM DRAPE											
Oil Lamp											900 MMG
CHRYSANTHEMUM DRAPE VARIANT											
Oil Lamp									950		
CHRYSANTHEMUM LEAF											
Rose Bowl, very rare											1500 ICG
Wine, tall stemmed, very rare											1200 ICG
CIRCLED ROSE											
Plate, 7"	95										
CIRCLED STAR AND VINE (JAIN)											
Tumbler	150										
CIRCLE SCROLL (DUGAN)											
Bowl, 5"	40	45									
Bowl, 10"	65	80									
Butter or Sugar	375	425									
Compote, scarce		225									
Creamer or Spooner	95	175									
Hat shape, scarce	60	95									
Pitcher, rare	1600	2200									
Tumbler, very scarce	350	425									
Vase Whimsey, scarce	135	265									300 BA
CLASSIC ARTS											
Powder Jar	400										
Rose Bowl	450										
Vase, 7½", very scarce	425										
CLEOPATRA											
Bottle	110										
CLEVELAND MEMORIAL (MILLERSBURG)											
Ashtray, rare	15000	7000									
COAL BUCKET											
Novelty	75										
COARSE RIB (HEISEY)											
Mustard Jar w/lid	200										
COBBLESTONE (IMPERIAL)											
Bowl, 8½"	135	300	125	500							550LV

Pattern Name	M	A	G	B	PO	AO	IB	IG	W	Red	Other
Plate, rare		1300									
COIN DOT (FENTON)											
Bowl, 6" – 10"	30	50	50	45		150				1000	100LV
Plate, 9", rare	200			260							
Rose Bowl	100	150	175	140						1450	
COIN DOT VARIANT (FENTON)											
Bowl	35	45	55	50							
COIN SPOT (DUGAN)											
Compote	45	80	70	100	175	375		350			
Goblet, rare								500			
COLOGNE BOTTLE (CAMBRIDGE)											
One size, rare	600		850								
COLONIAL (IMPERIAL)											
Child's Mug, handled	65										
Lemonade Goblet	40										
Open Creamer or Sugar	30										
COLONIAL ALMOND (MCKEE)											
Bowl	125										
COLONIAL DECANTER											
Decanter w/stopper	250										
COLONIAL LADY (IMPERIAL)											
Vase, scarce	1000	750									
COLONIAL LOOP											
Wine	150										
COLONIAL TULIP (NORTHWOOD)											
Compote, plain			65								
Compote, rayed interior			80								85 TL
COLORADO (U.S. GLASS)											
*Exterior pattern only											
COLUMBIA (IMPERIAL)											
Cake Plate, scarce	125										75 CM
Compote	60	300	225								85 SM
Rose Bowl, rare	200										
Vase	45	125	165								110 SM
COLUMBIA VARIANT (IMPERIAL)											
Compote, scarce	75										
COLUMBUS											
Plate, 8"	45										
COLUMNS AND RINGS											
Hat Whimsey	65										
COMPASS (DUGAN)											
Exterior only											
COMPOTE VASE (FENTON)											
Stemmed Whimsey	50	65	70	75							
COMPOTE VASE VARIANT (FENTON)											
Compote, stemmed		75									
CONCAVE COLUMNS											
Vase, very rare						3500					
CONCAVE DIAMOND (FENTON)											
Vase											125 V
CONCAVE DIAMONDS (NORTHWOOD)											
Coaster, not iridized											65 CeB
Pickle Caster, complete	750										175 V
Pitcher w/lid			450 RG								300 CeB
Tumbler			400 RG								60 CeB
Tumble-up, complete, rare			115 OG								155 RG
Vase											200 CeB
CONCAVE FLUTE (WESTMORELAND)											
Banana Bowl	65	85									100 AM
Bowl	45	55	65								75 TL
Plate, 8½" – 9", rare		135									
Rose Bowl	60	95	100								
Vase	40	65	65								90 IM
CONCORD (FENTON)											
Bowl, 9"	225	275	550	300							400 AM
Plate, 10", rare	1900	2400	4900								3500 AM
CONE AND TIE (IMPERIAL)											
Tumbler, very rare		2000									
CONNIE (NORTHWOOD)											
Pitcher									750		
Tumbler									150		
CONSOLIDATED SHADE											
Shade, 16", rare											500 MMG
CONSTELLATION (DUGAN)											
Compote	85	450			400				100		425 LV
CONTINENTAL BOTTLE											
Two sizes	40										
COOLEEMEE, N.C. (FENTON)											
Plate, advertising, rare											
(J. N. LEDFORD)	9000										
CORAL (FENTON)											
Bowl, 9"	325		225	500					400		
Plate, 9½", rare	1350										
CORINTH (DUGAN)											
Banana Boat	55	75			150						

Pattern Name	M	A	G	B	PO	AO	IB	IG	W	Red	Other
Bowl, 9"	40	50			125						
Plate, 8½", rare					225						
Vase	30	40			150						200 AM
CORINTH (WESTMORELAND)											
Bowl	40	60									75 TL
Lamp, scarce		250									
Vase	30	50	75		150	550 BO					220 BO
CORN BOTTLE (IMPERIAL)											
One size, scarce	375		350								465 SM
CORN CRUET											
One size, rare									1100		
CORNFLOWERS											
Bowl, footed	125										
CORNING INSULATOR (CORNING)											
Insulator, various shapes	35+										
CORNUCOPIA (JEANNETTE)											
Vase	40										
CORN VASE (NORTHWOOD)											
Regular Mold	1000	750	1000	2300		3250	2500	425	400		400 LG
Pulled Husk Variant, rare		16500	13000								
CORONATION (ENGLISH)											
Vase, 5" (Victoria Crown Design)	250										
CORONET											
Tumbler	30										
COSMOS (MILLERSBURG)											
Bowl, ice cream shaped	1650		85								
Bowl, six ruffles, scarce			125								
Bowl, eight ruffles, very scarce			200								
Plate, rare			525								
COSMOS (NORTHWOOD)											
Pitcher	265										
Tumbler	30										
COSMOS AND CANE (U.S. GLASS)											
Basket, two handled, rare											1000 HA
Bowl, 5" – 7"	40								145		50 HA
Bowl, 10"	75								235		95 HA
Breakfast Set, two pieces									475		165 HA
Butter, covered	175								300		400 HA
Chop Plate, rare	1200								1350		1300 HA
Compote, stemmed, tall	400								350		
Compote Whimsey	450								400		
Creamer or Spooner	65								200		75 HA
Flat Tray, rare									275		
Pitcher, rare	850								1950		1250 HA
Tumbler	75								150		95 HA
Tumbler, advertising, J.R. Millner, very scarce											250 HA
Rose Bowl, large	350	1200									1800 HA
Rose Bowl Whimsey	650	1500									
Spittoon Whimsey, rare									3000		4750 HA
Sugar w/lid	100								165		
Stemmed Dessert									150		
Whimsey, volcano shape	550								500		
COSMOS AND HOBSTAR											
Bowl (on metal stand)	450										
COSMOS VARIANT											
Bowl, 9" – 10"	40	65		75					125	775	700 AB
Plate, 10", rare	190	250			400				425		
COUNTRY KITCHEN (MILLERSBURG)											
Bowl, 5", very scarce	90										
Bowl, 8", very scarce	175										
Bowl, 10", very scarce	295										
Bowl, square, rare	500										
Covered Butter, rare	650	900									
Creamer or Spooner	300	350	750								
Spittoon Whimsey, rare		4650									
Sugar w/lid	325	400	800								
Vase Whimsey, two sizes, rare	850	1350									2000 V
COURTESY											
Bowl, 3¼"	25	55									
COURT HOUSE (MILLERSBURG)											
Bowl, lettered, scarce		875									3500 LV
COURT HOUSE UNLETTERED VARIANT											
Bowl, unlettered, rare		4500									
COVERED FROG (COOPERATIVE FLINT)											
One Size	375	450					300	475	475		
COVERED HEN (ENGLISH)											
One size	350			500							
COVERED LITTLE HEN											
Miniature, 3½", rare											90 CM
COVERED MALLARD (U.S. GLASS)											
One Shape											450 CM
COVERED SWAN (ENGLISH)											
One Size	325	425		525							

Pattern Name	M	A	G	B	PO	AO	IB	IG	W	Red	Other
CRAB CLAW (IMPERIAL)											
Bowl, 5"	25	35	40								65 SM
Bowl, 8" – 10"	50	125	95								75 SM
CRAB CLAW VARIANT (IMPERIAL)											
Pitcher	275										
Tumbler	35										
CRACKLE (IMPERIAL)											
Bowl, 5"	15	20	20								
Bowl, 9"	25	30	30								
Candy Jar w/lid	30										
Candlestick, 3½"	25										
Candlestick, 7"	30										
Plate, 6" – 8"	25										
Punch Bowl and Base	55										
Punch Cup	10										
Pitcher, dome base	90										
Tumbler, dome base	20										
Salt Shaker											60 AQ
Sherbet	20										
Spittoon, large	50										
Wall Vase	40										
Window Planter, rare	110										
CRACKLE (JEANNETTE)											
Auto Vase	25										
Bowl, 8"	25										
CRACKLE SHAKER SET											
Shakers in Metal Holder	125										
CR ASHTRAY (ARGENTINA)											
Ashtray	175		450	350							400 AM
CREOLE											
Rose Bowl, stemmed, rare	1500										
CROSSHATCH (SOWERBY)											
Creamer	75										
Sugar, open	75										
CROWN OF DIAMONDS (CRYSTAL)											
*Exterior of Trailing Flowers											
CROWN OF INDIA (JAIN)											
Tumbler	250										
CRUCIFIX (IMPERIAL)											
Candlestick, each, rare	600										
CRYSTAL DIAMONDS (CRYSTAL)											
Bowl	65										
CUBA (MCKEE)											
Goblet, rare	50										
CURTAIN OPTIC (FENTON)											
Pitcher											450 V
Tumbler											150 V
Tumble-up, complete											350 V
CURVED STAR/ CATHEDRAL											
Bowl, 3½"	25										
Bowl, 10"	50										
Bowl, square, 7¾"	175										
Butterdish, two sizes	275										
Chalice, 7"	100			200							
Compote, two sizes	60										
Creamer, footed	60										
Epergne, scarce	325										
Flower Holder	135										
Pitcher, rare				3200							
Rose Bowl, scarce	200			400							
Vase, 9½", rare	325	475		875							
CUT ARCHES (ENGLISH)											
Banana Bowl	80										
CUT ARCS (FENTON)											
Bowl, 7½" – 10"	50		120								250 V
Compote	55	60		55							
Vase Whimsey (from bowl)	40	50	150	50						75	
CUT COSMOS											
Tumbler, rare	250										
CUT CRYSTAL (U.S. GLASS)											
Compote, 5½"	110										
Water Bottle	185										
CUT DAHLIA (JENKINS)											
Flower Basket	185										
CUT DIAMOND DECANTER											
Decanter with clear stopper	100										
CUT FLOWERS											
Vase, 10"	125										140 SM
CUT GRAPE MINI TUMBLER											
Miniature Tumbler, 3"	75										
CUT GRECIAN GOLD (FENTON)											
Lamp Font	100										
CUT OVALS (FENTON)											
Bowl, 7" – 10"	60									350	75 SM
Candlesticks, each	135									800	210 SM

Pattern Name	M	A	G	B	PO	AO	IB	IG	W	Red	Other
CUT OVALS (RIIHIMAKI)											
Butter											300 AM
CUT PRISMS (RINDSKOPF)											
Bowl, 6¼", scarce	60										
CUT SPRAYS (IMPERIAL)											
Vase, 10½"	45										175 IM
CUT STARS											
Shot Glass, 2"	50										
CZECH FLOWER											
Cruet	200										
CZECH INTERIOR COIN SPOT											
Vase, 12"											65 PB
CZECH INTERIOR SWIRL											
Lemonade Pitcher	175										
Lemonade Tumbler	25										
CZECHOSLOVAKIAN											
Liquor Set, complete	350										
Pitcher	350										
Tumbler	100										
(All pieces have black enameling)											
CZECH SWIRLS											
Tumbler w/enameling	90										
DAGNY (SWEDEN)											
Vase	300			350							
DAHLIA (DUGAN)											
Bowl, footed, 5"	40	65							95		
Bowl, footed, 10"	95	225							225		
Butter	120	155							350		
Creamer or Spooner	75	90							125		
Sugar	90	100							200		
Sundae, flared, rare	150										
Pitcher, rare (old only)	500	725							800		
Tumbler, rare (old only)	90	185							175		
DAHLIA (FENTON)											
Twist Epergne, One Lily	325								325		
DAHLIA											
Button		20									
DAHLIA (JENKINS)											
Compote, very scarce	150										
Vase, 10", rare	200										
DAHLIA AND DRAPE (FENTON)											
Tumble-Up, complete	150										
DAINTY BUD VASE											
One size	55										
DAINTY FLOWER											
Vase, 5", with enameled design		75								125	
DAISIES AND DIAMONDS											
Bowl, 9"	90										
DAISY (FENTON)											
Bonbon, scarce	125			200							
DAISY AND CANE (BROCKWITZ)											
Bowl, footed	50										
Bowl, oval, 12"	90										
Decanter, rare	100										
Epergne	175										
Pitcher, rare	1575										
Salver	80										
Spittoon, rare	1400			1275							
Vase, scarce	175										
Wine, very scarce	125										
DAISY AND DIAMOND POINT											
Bowl, rare	150										
DAISY AND DRAPE (NORTHWOOD)											
Vase	575	600	3200	900		700	2200	3500	210		700 LV
DAISY AND LITTLE FLOWERS (NORTHWOOD)											
Pitcher				300							
Tumbler				40							
DAISY AND PLUME (DUGAN)											
Candy Dish, three footed	65	140			200						325 LG
Bowl, footed, 8" – 9", Cherry Interior, rare		600									
DAISY AND PLUME (NORTHWOOD)											
Candy Dish, three footed	50	135	75				600	800	350		650 LG
Compote, stemmed, plain interior	45	75	60								300 AM
Compote, tricorner top, very scarce			150								
Rose Bowl, stemmed	40	90	110	375							225 AM
Rose Bowl, three footed	70	130	110	425		6000	1200	1000	750		1250 AQ
*Some have Northwood's Fern interior											
DAISY AND PLUME BANDED (NORTHWOOD)											
Compote or Rose Bowl, stemmed	85	100									125 PHO
DAISY AND SCROLL											
Decanter w/stopper	250										
Wine	75										
DAISY BASKET (IMPERIAL)											
One Size	65										75 CM

Pattern Name	M	A	G	B	PO	AO	IB	IG	W	Red	Other
DAISY BLOCK (ENGLISH)											
Row Boat, scarce	225	325									
DAISY CHAIN											
Shade	50										
DAISY CUT BELL (FENTON)											
One size, scarce	350										
DAISY DEAR (DUGAN)											
Bowl	20	45			60				85		100 AQ
Whimsey, J.I.P., scarce	65										
Whimsey Plate, rare					275						
DAISY DRAPES											
Vase, 6¼"	60										
DAISY DRAPE VASE (INDIA)											
Vase	225										
DAISY MAY											
* Exterior pattern only											
DAISY IN OVAL PANELS (U.S. GLASS)											
Creamer or Sugar	55										
DAISY ROSE (LADY FINGERS)											
Vase, 8"	175										
DAISY SPRAY											
Vase	65										
DAISY SQUARES											
Celery Vase Whimsey	600										
Compote, various shapes, rare	575										900 LG
Goblet, rare	600	750									750 V
Rose Bowl, scarce	475		600					625			
DAISY WEB (DUGAN)											
Hat, very scarce	300	675			750						
DAISY WREATH (WESTMORELAND)											
Bowl, 8" – 10"	175	250			200	300					225 BO
Vase, very rare	500										
DANCE OF THE VEILS (FENTON)											
Centerpiece bowl, very rare									5500		
Vase, very rare	12000										
DANDELION (NORTHWOOD)											
Mug	125	200	550	325		750					750 BO
Mug (Knight Templar), rare	300						650	800			
Pitcher	475	650	1200				7000	30000	7500		
Tumbler	45	70	105				135	300	125		245 LV
Vase Whimsey, rare		850									
DART											
Oil Lamp, rare	500										
DAVANN											
Vase, 8" – 9", scarce	175										
DAVENPORT											
Lemonade Tumbler	35										
DAVISONS SOCIETY CHOCOLATES											
Plate, handgrip		1000									
DECO											
Vase, scarce	275										
DECO LILY											
Bulbous Vase	400										
DECORAMA											
Pitcher	550										
Tumbler	175										
DEEP GRAPE (MILLERSBURG)											
Compote, rare	1800	2200	2000	7000							
Compote, ruffled top, rare		2500									
Rose Bowl, stemmed, rare			8000								
DELORES											
Perfume	60										
DELTA BASE (IMPERIAL)											
Candlesticks, pair	150										
DESERT GODDESS											
Epergne			475								500 AM
DE SVENSKA											
Vase 11½"				200							
DEVILBISS											
Atomizer, complete	100										
Perfumer	65										
DEWHIRST BERRY BAND											
Carafe, 7"	175										
Compote	85										
DIAGONAL BAND											
Tankard, scarce	675	550									
DIAGONAL RIDGE											
Pitcher	50										
Tumbler	10										
DIAMANTES STAR (JAIN)											
Vase	450										
DIAMOND (CRYSTAL)											
Creamer	60	80									
Sugar, open	70	85									

Pattern Name	M	A	G	B	PO	AO	IB	IG	W	Red	Other
DIAMOND AND BOWS (DIAMOND AND GRAPES)											
Tumbler	200										
DIAMOND AND DAISY CUT (U.S. GLASS)											
Pitcher, rare	400			450							
Tumbler, 4", very scarce	65			95							
Tumbler, 5", rare	150										
Vase, square, 10"	225										
DIAMOND AND DAISY CUT VARIANT (JENKINS)											
Punch Bowl w/base, rare	625										
DIAMOND AND FAN											
Compote					100						
Cordial Set, seven pieces	350										
DIAMOND AND FAN (MILLERSBURG)											
Exterior pattern only											
DIAMOND AND FAN WITH WASHBOARD PANELS											
Shakers, each	35										
DIAMOND AND FILE (FENTON)											
Bowl, 7" – 9"	45										
Plate, two sides up, 9½", scarce	150										
DIAMOND AND RIB (FENTON)											
Jardiniere Whimsey	1400	1600	2000	1600							
Vase, 7" – 12"	20	60	60	100					155		75 SM
Vase, funeral, 17" – 22"	2300	1650	1650	1900					800		
Vase Whimsey, spittoon shape			1800								
DIAMOND AND SUNBURST (IMPERIAL)											
Decanter w/stopper	125	325									
Oil Cruet, rare			900								
Wine	55	60									
DIAMOND ARCHES											
Bowl	85										
DIAMOND BAND (CRYSTAL)											
Float Set, scarce	400	550									
Open Sugar	45	60									
DIAMOND BAND AND FAN (ENGLISH)											
Cordial set, complete, rare	900										
DIAMOND BLOCK (IMPERIAL)											
Candlestick	60										45 CM
Compote	45										35 CM
Cylinder Vase, 10" and 12", rare	425										
Light Shade	40			125							70 SM
Milk Pitcher	90										85 CM
Rose Bowl	65										50 CM
Tumbler, small juice size	30										25 CM
Vase, 8½", footed	80										135 SM
DIAMOND CANE											
Sugar Box	165										
DIAMOND CATTAILS (INDIA)											
Tumbler	225										
DIAMOND CHAIN											
Bowl, 6¼"	60										
DIAMOND CHECKERBOARD											
Bowl, 5"	25										
Bowl, 9"	40										
Butter	90										
Cracker Jar	85										
Tumbler	100										
DIAMOND COLLAR (INDIANA GLASS)											
Bowl	65										
DIAMOND CUT											
Banana Bowl	90	115									
Bowl, 10"	90	150									
Compote	75										
Rose Bowl, 9½", rare	175	425									
DIAMOND CUT SHIELDS											
Pitcher	475										
Tumbler	125										
DIAMOND DAISY											
Plate, 8"	95										
DIAMOND FLOWER											
Compote, miniature	85										
DIAMOND FOUNTAIN (HIGBEE)											
Bowl, scarce	100										
Cruet, very scarce	425										
Plate, handgrip, rare	250										
DIAMOND HEART											
Vase, 5½"	70										
DIAMOND HONEYCOMB											
Sugar w/lid	85			200							

Pattern Name	M	A	G	B	PO	AO	IB	IG	W	Red	Other
DIAMOND LACE (IMPERIAL)											
Bowl, 5"	25	30	50								
Bowl, 10" – 11"	65	110	250								
Bowl, 10", ice cream shape, scarce											110 CM
Pitcher		375									
Tumbler	190	50							250		
Rose Bowl Whimsey, very rare	2000										
DIAMOND OVALS (ENGLISH)											
Bottle and Stopper	100										
Compote (open sugar)	40										
Creamer	40										
Plate, stemmed	150										
DIAMOND PANELS AND RIBS (INDIA)											
Tumbler	175										
DIAMOND PINWHEEL (ENGLISH)											
Bowl, 10⅞"	60										
Butter	90										
Compote	45										
DIAMOND POINT (NORTHWOOD)											
Vase, 7" – 14"	30	85	110	250		1300	800	425			300 SA
Vase w/original label		2500									
DIAMOND POINT COLUMNS (FENTON)											
Banana Bowl, scarce	80										
Bowl, 5"	25										
Bowl, 7½"	35										
Plate, 7", scarce	55										
Vase	40	100	75	90							125 V
DIAMOND POINT COLUMNS (LATE)											
Bowl, 5"	20										
Bowl, 9"	30										
Compote	35										
Butter	40										
Creamer, Spooner, or Sugar	30										
Powder Jar w/lid	40										
Milk Pitcher	50										
DIAMOND POINTS (NORTHWOOD)											
Basket, rare	1400	2100		2500					2800		
DIAMOND POINTS VARIANT (FOSTORIA)											
Rose Bowl, rare	1200										
DIAMOND PRISMS											
Basket	75										
Compote	55										
DIAMOND RAIN											
Tumbler, scarce	150										
DIAMOND RING (IMPERIAL)											
Bowl, 5"	25	30									30 SM
Bowl, 9"	40	50									55 SM
Fruit Bowl, 9½"	65	90									65 SM
Rose Bowl, scarce	250	425									325 SM
DIAMONDS (MILLERSBURG)											
Pitcher	275	385	425								525 TL
Tumbler	65	90	80								175 TL
Punch Bowl and Base, rare	3200	5500	4000								
Pitcher (no spout), rare		600	600								
Spittoon Whimsey, very rare	4500										
DIAMOND SHIELD											
Compote	150										
DIAMOND SPARKLER (U.S. GLASS)											
Vase, very rare	250										
DIAMOND'S ROYAL LUSTRE											
Candlesticks, pair	80	125		175				125		300	
Console Bowl	55	70		85				60		135	
DIAMOND'S SODA GOLD											
Exterior pattern only											
DIAMOND STORM											
Tumbler, scarce	125										
DIAMOND STUD (INDIA)											
Pitcher	325										
Tumbler	150										
DIAMOND STUDS											
Spittoon Whimsey, rare			350								
DIAMOND STAR											
Mug, two sizes	125										
Vase, 8"	80										
DIAMOND THUMBPRINT											
Mini Oil Lamp, 6½"	250										
DIAMOND TOP (ENGLISH)											
Creamer	40										
Spooner	40										
DIAMOND VANE (ENGLISH)											
Creamer, 4"	35										
DIAMOND WEDGE (JENKINS)											
Pickle Caster in holder with fork	165										

Pattern Name	M	A	G	B	PO	AO	IB	IG	W	Red	Other
Tumbler	85										
DIAMOND WHEEL											
Bowl	75										
DIAMOND WITH FAN PANELED											
Shakers, each	40										
DIAMOND WITH THUMBPRINT BAND											
Shakers, each	40										
DIANA, THE HUNTRESS											
Bowl, 8"	350										
DIANTHUS (FENTON)											
Pitcher								475	500		
Tumbler								60	65		
DIMPLES (INDIA)											
Vase	225										
DINOSAUR (RINDSKOPF)											
Bowl, 8" – 9"	2500										
DIPLOMAT (FENTON)											
Tumbler, rare	165										
DIVING DOLPHINS (ENGLISH)											
Bowl, footed, 7"	225	275	425	325							
Rose Bowl, scarce	325	475									
Whimsey Bowl, rare											600 AQ
DOG											
Ashtray	90										
DOG AND DEER											
Decanter, enameled	250										
Shot Glass, enameled	75										
DOGWOOD SPRAYS (DUGAN)											
Bowl, 9"	150	250		350	225						325 BO
Compote	175	225			250						
DOLPHINS (MILLERSBURG)											
Compote, rare		2300	4000	5700							
DORIA											
Gravy Boat w/underplate	200										
DOROTHY											
Perfume	50										
DORSEY AND FUNKENSTEIN (FENTON)											
Bowl, advertising, very scarce		1100									
Plate, advertising, very scarce		2600									
DOT											
Vase, 5¼", rare		350									
DOTTED DAISIES											
Plate, 8"	90										
DOTTED DIAMONDS AND DAISIES											
Pitcher	175										
Tumbler	55										
DOUBLE BANDED FLUTE											
Vase, 9"	125										
DOUBLE CROSSROADS											
Shakers, each		140	125								
DOUBLE DAISY (FENTON)											
Pitcher, bulbous	200										
Pitcher, tankard	250		385								
Tumbler	30		40								
DOUBLE DIAMOND (BROCKWITZ)											
Cologne Bottle, two sizes	125 – 175										
Covered Puff Box, two sizes	100 – 140										
Perfume with Atomizer	145										
Ring Tray	95										
Ring Tree	100										
Tumbler	125										
Tumble-up	175										
Waste Bowl	90										
DOUBLE DIAMONDS											
Cologne	90										
Pin Tray	60										
Puff Box	50										
Perfume	80										
Ring Tree	85										
Tumble-up	110										
DOUBLE DOLPHIN (FENTON)											
Bowl, flat, 8" – 10"											65 CeB
Bowl, footed, 9" – 11"											115 CeB
Cake Plate, center handled											85 CeB
Candlesticks, pair											90 CeB
Compote											70 CeB
Covered Candy, stemmed											80 CeB
Fan Vase											90 CeB
DOUBLE DUTCH (IMPERIAL)											
Bowl, footed, 9"	50	180	75								85 SM
DOUBLE LOOP (NORTHWOOD)											
Creamer	175	200	250	425		600					
Sugar	55	100	150	100		300					
DOUBLE RING SHOT											
Shot Glass	35										

Pattern Name	M	A	G	B	PO	AO	IB	IG	W	Red	Other
DOUBLE SCROLL (IMPERIAL)											
Bowl, console	50									250	425 V
Candlesticks, pair	75									400	275 V
DOUBLE STAR (CAMBRIDGE)											
Bowl, 9", rare			400								
Pitcher, scarce	600	700	450								
Tumbler, scarce	275	225	65								
Spittoon Whimsey, rare			3900								
DOUBLE STEM ROSE (DUGAN)											
Bowl, dome base, 8½"	45	200		195	175			1750			600 CeB
Plate, footed, scarce	200	350			285				165		
DOUBLE STIPPLED RAYS											
Bowl											85 AM
DOUGHNUT BRIDLE ROSETTE											
One Size		95									
A DOZEN ROSES (IMPERIAL)											
Bowl, footed, 8" – 10", scarce	500	900	1400								
Advertising Ashtray, various designs	60+										
DRAGON AND LOTUS (FENTON)											
Banana Bowl, very rare	1800										
Bowl, flat, 9"	55	155	190	100	700	2850				2250	1000 AT-O
Bowl, footed, 9"	90	195	175	150	250					2200	185 SM
Nut Bowl, scarce				425							
Plate, 9½"	2000	2500		2500	2900					7000	
DRAGON AND STRAWBERRY (FENTON)											
Bowl, flat, 9", scarce	500	3500	1500	1600							
Bowl, footed, 9", scarce	400		1700	950							
Plate (Absentee Dragon), rare	6000										
DRAGONFLY											
Shade											65 AM
DRAGONFLY LAMP											
Oil Lamp, rare								1900	1400		1800 PK
DRAGON'S TONGUE (FENTON)											
Bowl, 11", scarce	1200										
Shade	225										150 MMG
DRAGON VASE											
Vase, with dragons, very rare				1200							1200 BA
DRAPE AND TASSEL											
Shade	45										
DRAPED ARCS (BROCKWITZ)											
Bowl				125							
DRAPERY (NORTHWOOD)											
Candy Dish	80	135	375	165			125	225	135		300 V
Rose Bowl	225	165		250		225	475	700	725		3000 ReB
Vase	90	250	325	350		550	325	225	175		1500 SA
*Add 10% for rose bowls crimped on ribs											
DRAPERY BRACELET (INDIA)											
Pitcher	350										
Tumbler	165										
DRAPERY ROSE (INDIA)											
Vase	175										
DRAPERY VARIANT (FENTON)											
Pitcher, rare	525										
Tumbler, scarce	200										
DRAPERY VARIANT (FINLAND)											
Pitcher	600										
Tumbler	200										
Shot Glass	225										
DRAPERY VARIANT (NORTHWOOD)											
Vase, scarce	85	200	550	175							350 LV
DREIBUS PARFAIT SWEETS (NORTHWOOD)											
Plate, two or four sides up		725									
Plate, flat, rare		900									
DRESSER BOTTLE SET											
Complete, five bottles w/holder	250										
DUCKIE											
Powder Jar w/lid	20										
DUCK SALT DIP											
Novelty Salt Dip	60										
DUGAN-DIAMOND'S RAINBOW											
Candy Jar w/lid, footed	55		75	85							
DUGAN'S #1013R											
Vase, 8" – 13"	50	75			85						
DUGAN'S FLUTE											
Vase, 7" – 13"	45	60									
DUGAN'S FRIT											
Vase, pinched					175						
DUGAN'S HYACINTH											
Vase	75				175						
Vase Whimsey, pinched, three sides	95	225			300						350 CeB
DUGAN'S MANY RIBS											
Hat Shape	30	40		75	95						
Vase	60	80		75	125						

Pattern Name	M	A	G	B	PO	AO	IB	IG	W	Red	Other
DUGAN'S PLAIN JANE											
Interior pattern on some Leaf Rosette and Beads bowls and plates											
DUGAN'S STIPPLED RAYS											
Bowl	35	45	50								
Hat	25	35	45								
DUGAN'S TRUMPET											
Vase, 14" – 16", very scarce	60										300 CeB
DUGAN'S TWIST											
Bowl		75									
DUGAN'S VENETIAN											
Rose Bowl		125		200							225 LV
Vase, various shapes and sizes	90	75	100	185	125						200 V
DUGAN'S VENETIAN HONEYCOMB											
Either shape		90		110							
DUGAN'S VINTAGE VARIANT											
Bowl, footed, 8½"	85	175	250	200							900 CeB
Plate	300	575									
DUNCAN (NATIONAL GLASS)											
Cruet	600										
DURAND ADVERTISMENT (FENTON)											
Orange Bowl, footed, (Grape and Cable w/advertising), very scarce				1600							
DUTCH MILL											
Ashtray	65										
Plate, 8"	50										
DUTCH PLATE											
One size, 8"	45										
DUTCH TWINS											
Ashtray	50										
DUTCH WINDMILL ASHTRAY											
Ashtray	40										
EAGLE FURNITURE (NORTHWOOD)											
Handgrip Plate, two sides up		900									
Handgrip Plate, one side up		750									
Plate, Advertising		1100									
E.A. HUDSON FURNITURE (NORTHWOOD)											
Bowl, rare, advertising		1500									
Plate, flat, advertising		1700									
Plate, handgrip, advertising		1300									
EARLY AMERICAN (DUNCAN AND MILLER)											
Plate	75										
EASTERN STAR (IMPERIAL)											
Exterior on some Scroll Embossed compotes											
EBON											
Vase		110 BA									
EGG AND DART											
Candlesticks, pair	90										
EGYPTIAN LUSTRE (DUGAN)											
Bowl		75 BA									
Plate		85 BA									
Vase		100 BA									
EGYPTIAN QUEEN'S VASE											
Vase, 7"	425										
ELEGANCE											
Bowl, 8¼", rare	2800						3000				
Plate, rare							3400				
ELEGANCE											
Pitcher, enameled, rare	800										
Tumbler, enameled, rare	350										
ELEKTRA											
Butter	150										
Compote, 4½"	50	60		65							
Creamer	70										
Sugar, open	65										
ELEPHANT PAPERWEIGHT											
Novelty Paperweight	300										
ELEPHANT'S FOOT VASE											
See Tree Trunk (Northwood)											
ELEPHANT VASE (JAIN)											
Vase, three sizes	110										
ELEPHANT VASE VARIANTS											
Vase	125										
ELKS (DUGAN)											
Nappy, very rare		7000									
ELKS (FENTON)											
Detroit Bowl, very scarce	9000	800	1100	1000							
Parkersburg Plate, rare			2000	2500							
Atlantic City Plate, rare			18000	1800							
Atlantic City Bowl, scarce				1300							
ELKS (MILLERSBURG)											
Bowl, rare		2500									

Pattern Name	M	A	G	B	PO	AO	IB	IG	W	Red	Other
ELKS PAPERWEIGHT (MILLERSBURG)											
Paperweight, rare		2500	6000								
ELYSIAN											
Vase, 9½"	350										
EMBROIDERED FLOWER AND URN (JAIN)											
Tumbler	90										
EMBROIDERED FLOWERS (JAIN)											
Tumbler	150										
EMBROIDERED MUMS (NORTHWOOD)											
Bowl, 9"	300	350		850		11000	800	950			250 LV
Plate				8000			1300	1700	2100		
Stemmed Bonbon									1000		
EMBROIDERED PANELS (JAIN)											
Spittoon (lamp base)	450										
Tumbler	165										
EMMA'S VASE											
Vase	400										
EMU (CRYSTAL)											
Bowl, 5", rare	150	175									
Bowl, 10", rare	900										1400 AM
Compote Variant, rare	700	850									
ENAMELED BLOSSOM SPRAY (DUGAN)											
Bowl, decorated					100						
Plate, decorated					120						
Handgrip Plate, decorated					145						
ENAMELED CHERRIES (OR GRAPES) NORTHWOOD											
Pitcher				225							
Tumbler				60							
ENAMELED CHRYSANTHEMUM											
Pitcher	140			195							
Tumbler	25			40							
ENAMELED CHRYSANTHEMUM WITH PRISM BAND											
Pitcher	165	225	225	200				265	200		
Tumbler	30	45	45	35				50	40		
ENAMELED COLUMBINE (FENTON)											
Pitcher	250	325	350	450							
Tumbler	30	40	55	60							
ENAMELED CORAL											
Pitcher	200										
ENAMELED CROCUS											
Pitcher	125			175					165		
Tumbler	20			35					30		
ENAMELED CROCUS VARIANT											
Pitcher	130			185					175		
Tumbler	25			40					35		
ENAMELED CROCUS W/PRISM BAND											
Pitcher	145			200					180		
Tumbler	30			45					35		
ENAMELED CRUET											
Cruet, with bird decoration	100										
ENAMELED DIAMOND POINT											
Bottle	100										
ENAMELED DOGWOOD											
Pitcher	400										
Tumbler	50										
ENAMELED DOUBLE DAISY											
Pitcher	130			165					170		
Tumbler	20			30					30		
ENAMELED FLORAL SPRAY											
Pitcher											500 CL
Tumbler											90 CL
ENAMELED FLOWERS CRUET											
Cruet, decorated	100										
ENAMELED FORGET-ME-NOT (FENTON)											
Pitcher	400		600	450							
Tumbler	45		75	60							
ENAMELED FREESIA											
Pitcher	125			190							
Tumbler	25			30							
ENAMELED GOOSEBERRY (NORTHWOOD)											
Tumbler				80							
ENAMELED GRAPE BAND											
Tumbler	50										
ENAMELED HONEYSUCKLE											
Tumbler	250										
ENAMELED IRIS (FENTON)											
Pitcher	550	700	1000	650							

Pattern Name	M	A	G	B	PO	AO	IB	IG	W	Red	Other
Tumbler	40	50	65	55							
ENAMELED LILY OF THE VALLEY											
Bowl, 8½"					100						
ENAMELED LOTUS (FENTON)											
Pitcher	225		325					450			
ENAMELED PANEL											
Goblet	190										
ENAMELED PERIWINKLE											
Pitcher	150										
Tumbler	25										
ENAMELED PHLOX											
Pitcher		275									
Tumbler		40									
ENAMELED PRISM BAND											
Pitcher	200	350	375	300				450	365		
Tumbler	45	55	65	55				85	55		
ENAMELED PUNTY BAND											
Tumbler, rare	325										
ENAMELED ROSE OF PARADISE											
Tumbler			200								
ENAMELED STIPPLED PETALS											
Bowl, 8½"					150						
ENAMELED STORK (GERMAN)											
Pitcher	175										
Tumbler	50										
ENAMELED SWALLOW											
Tankard Pitcher w/lid	225										
Tumbler	50										
ENAMELED WINDFLOWER											
Tumbler	75										
ENCORE											
Bottle (late)	10										
ENCRUSTED VINE											
Tumbler	25										
ENGLISH BUTTON BAND (ENGLISH)											
Creamer	45										
Sugar	45										
ENGLISH FLUTE AND FILE (SOWERBY)											
Compote	70										120 LV
Creamer or Sugar	45										70 LV
ENGLISH HOB AND BUTTON (ENGLISH)											
Bowl, 7" – 10"	60	80	95	70							
Epergne (metal base)	125			145							
ENGLISH HOBNAIL (WESTMORELAND)											
Toilet Bottle											125 CRAN
ENGLISH HOBSTAR											
Oval Bowl, 6", in holder	150										
ENGRAVED CORNFLOWER (FENTON)											
Pitcher, scarce	450										
Tumbler, scarce	75										
ENGRAVED DAISY											
Tumbler, scarce	40										
ENGRAVED DAISY AND SPEARS											
Goblet, 4½"	75										
ENGRAVED FLORAL (FENTON)											
Tumbler			95								
ENGRAVED GRAPES (FENTON)											
Candy Jar w/lid	85										
Juice Glass	30										
Pitcher, squat	120										
Pitcher, tall	145										
Tumbler	30										
Tumble-up	150										
Vase	65										
ENGRAVED ZINNIA (FENTON)											
Tumbler	50										
ESBERARD-RIO											
Plate, rare	250										
ESTATE (WESTMORELAND)											
Bud Vase, 6"	50										
Creamer or Sugar	55										75 SM
Mug, rare	75				75	210 BO					110 AQ
Perfume, very scarce											400 SM
ETCHED BUTTERFLY (IMPERIAL)											
Vase	135										
ETCHED CIGARETTE BOX											
Box with cover	125										
ETCHED DECO (STANDARD)											
Bowl, three footed, 7"	35										
Creamer	45										
Hat Shape	45										

Pattern Name	M	A	G	B	PO	AO	IB	IG	W	Red	Other
Nappy, handled	40										
Plate, three footed, 8"	50										
Plate, pedestal footed, 8"	60										
Variant Plate (no etching)	55										
ETCHED GARDEN MUMS											
Plate		200									
ETCHED LEAVES											
Oil Bottle, 6⅞"	80										
ETCHED VINE											
Tumbler	40										
ETCHED VINE AND FLOWERS (INDIA)											
Pitcher	425										
Tumbler	135										
EURO											
Vase w/brass top	45										
EURO DIAMONDS											
Berry Bowl, small			15								
Berry Bowl, large			45								
EUROPA											
Vase, 9¾"	40										
EUROPEAN POPPY											
Butter											165 AM
EUROPEAN VINTAGE GRAPE											
Bowl, 8", rare	400										
EVELYN (FOSTORIA)											
Bowl (1940s)			1000								
EXCHANGE BANK (FENTON)											
Bowl, advertising		800									
Plate, advertising, 6"		1700									
Plate, advertising, handgrip		1600									
EXOTIC LUSTRE											
Lemonade Tumbler, scarce	50										
EYE CUP											
One size	90										
FAMOUS											
Puff Box	75										
FAN (DUGAN)											
Bowl, Sauce, 5"	40	55			100						
Gravy Boat, footed	65	180			150						
FANCIFUL (DUGAN)											
Bowl, 8½"	125	350		550	275				110		350 LV
Plate, 9"	200	625		775	550				225		950 LV
FANCY (NORTHWOOD)											
Interior on some Fine Cut and Roses pieces											
FANCY CORN HUSK VASE (DUGAN)											
Corn Vase, rare	1300										
FANCY CUT (ENGLISH)											
Miniature Pitcher, rare	225										
Miniature Tumbler, scarce	60										
FANCY FLOWERS (IMPERIAL)											
Compote	120		175								
FAN MONTAGE											
Biscuit Jar w/lid, rare	225										
FANS											
Cracker Jar (metal lid)	175										
Pitcher	300										
Tumbler	125										
FAN STAR (MILLERSBURG)											
Exterior only											
FAN-TAIL (FENTON)											
Bowl, footed, 9"	100		275	250					325		
Bowl, shallow ice cream shape, very scarce	200		400	325							
Plate, footed, rare	5600			6000							
FAN-TAIL MINI SHAKER SET											
Shaker Set, complete with holder	150										
FAR EASTERN											
Jar	135										
FARMYARD (DUGAN)											
Bowl, 10", scarce		7500	11000		13000						
Bowl, 10", square, very scarce		8250	12500								
Plate, 10½", very rare		18000									
FASHION (IMPERIAL)											
Bowl, 9"	40		90								55 SM
Bride's Basket	125										150 CM
Butter	75	200									
Compote	600										525 SM
Creamer or Sugar	25	145									100 SM
Punch Bowl w/base	175	1800									4000 SM
Punch Cup	10	40									60 SM
Pitcher	150	900									550 SM
Tumbler	20	300									85 SM
Rose Bowl, very rare	225	900	375								

Pattern Name	M	A	G	B	PO	AO	IB	IG	W	Red	Other
FEATHER AND HEART (MILLERSBURG)											
Pitcher, scarce	425	650	1000								14500 V
Tumbler, scarce	60	100	200								
Hair Receiver Whimsey, very rare	2000										
Spittoon Whimsey, very rare	7000										
FEATHER COLUMNS (INDIA)											
Tumbler	175										
FEATHERED ARROW											
Bowl, 8½" – 9½"	65										70 CM
Rose Bowl, rare	200										
FEATHERED FLOWERS											
Exterior only											
FEATHERED RAYS (FENTON)											
Bowl, rare			450								
FEATHERED SERPENT (FENTON)											
Bowl, 5"	30	40	45	40							
Bowl, 10"	90	75	90	65							
Bowl, 6", tricorner	70	110	130								
Spittoon Whimsey, rare		6000	7500								
FEATHERS (NORTHWOOD)											
Vase, 7" – 14"	45	85	75				200		400		
FEATHER SCROLL											
Sugar with lid	225										
Tumbler	80										
FEATHER STITCH (FENTON)											
Bowl, 8½" – 10"	80	125	175	125						7500	275 AQ
Plate (low bowl), scarce	950										
FEATHER SWIRL (U.S. GLASS)											
Butter	165										
Vase	65										
FELDMAN BROS (FENTON)											
Open Edge Basket	65										
FENTON FLUTE											
Vase	25	55	65	50					90	300	100 V
FENTONIA (FENTON)											
Bowl, footed, 5"	30	70	70	60							
Bowl, footed, 9½"	100	125	125	110							
Butter	115			185							
Creamer, Sugar, or Spooner	75			90							
Fruit Bowl, 10"	85			100							
Pitcher	400			625							
Tumbler	50			75							
Vase Whimsey, rare	325			450							
FENTONIA FRUIT (FENTON)											
Bowl, footed, 6"	60			120							
Bowl, footed, 10"	125			175							
Butter, very rare				1000							
Pitcher, rare	600			1200							
Tumbler, rare	200			475							
FENTON LEMON WEDGE SERVER											
One size	45							100	75		125 AM
FENTON'S #3											
Creamer	45										
Sugar, open	45										
FENTON'S #9											
Candy Jar w/lid	35										70 V
FENTON'S #232											
Candlesticks, each	40										110 CeB
FENTON'S #260											
Compote, 7"	40										75 CeB
FENTON'S #314											
Candlesticks, pair											200 WS
FENTON'S #568											
Candy Compote w/lid											125 IG
FENTON'S #574											
Vase/Compote, 6" and 12"	25 – 40		35 – 55								60 V
FENTON'S #631											
Plate, 9"											60 CeB
FENTON'S #643											
Compote	50										70 CeB
Covered Candy	70										95 CeB
Plate, 7"	35							40			
Rose Bowl	60										75 CeB
Salver	65							75			
FENTON'S #649											
Candlesticks											160 V
FENTON'S #736 ELITE											
Candy Jar	75										90 CeB
Compote	65										75 CeB
Rose Bowl, very scarce	175									300	225 CeB
FENTON'S # 847											
Bowl									65		
Candy Jar											125 AQ
Fan Vase								85			

Pattern Name	M	A	G	B	PO	AO	IB	IG	W	Red	Other
FENTON'S #888											
Vase	55			70							
FENTON'S #1502 (DIAMOND OPTIC DOLPHINS)											
Bonbon											125 AQ
Bowl											90 AQ
Compote											110 AQ
FENTON'S CHERRIES (FENTON)											
Banana Boat, very rare	3000			2750							
FENTON'S CORNUCOPIA											
Candlesticks, pair	75						195	100	85		
FENTON'S FLOWERS (FENTON)											
Nut Bowl	35	135	150	500					165		
Rose Bowl	45	125	150	100	1300				175	2200	300 V
Rose Bowl Variant, smooth top, rare				600							
FENTON'S PANELS											
Vase, 8" – 9"	30										
FENTON'S SMOOTH RAYS											
Bowl, 5" – 6"	25	35	40	45				55			
Bowl, tricorner, 6½"	30	45	50	55				70			
Bowl, square, 9", scarce	70		90								
FERN (FENTON)											
Bowl, 7" – 9", rare				1100							
FERN (NORTHWOOD)											
Compote	100	90	135				1400				
*(Daisy and Plume exterior)											
FERN AND WATTLE (CRYSTAL)											
*Exterior pattern only											
FERN BRAND CHOCOLATES (NORTHWOOD)											
Plate		1300									
FERN PANELS (FENTON)											
Hat	45		60	50						425	
FESTIVAL MOON (JAPAN) AKA: ID KA CHAND											
Tumbler, rare	150										
FIELD FLOWER (IMPERIAL)											
Milk Pitcher, rare	180	200	220								225 AM
Pitcher, scarce	165	550	450	2000							325 TL
Tumbler, scarce	35	60	70	350						1500	125 VI
FIELD THISTLE, (U.S. GLASS)											
Bowl, 6" – 10"	50						250				
Butter, rare	125										
Breakfast Set, two piece, rare							325				
Compote	150										
Plate, 6", rare	200										
Plate, 9", rare	300										
Pitcher, scarce	175										
Tumbler, scarce	45										
Sugar, Creamer, or Spooner, rare	100										
Vase, two sizes	250 – 500										
FILE (IMPERIAL)											
Bowl, 5"	30	40									
Bowl, 7" – 10"	45	50									60 CM
Compote	40	50									60 CM
Creamer or Spooner	85										
Juice Tumbler, rare	300										
Lemonade Tumbler (variant), rare	1000										
Pitcher, rare	300	500									
Tumbler, scarce	100										
Sugar	125										
Vase Whimsey, from sugar, scarce	350										
FILE (SOWERBY)											
Handled Sweetmeat Bowl	175										
FILE AND FAN											
Bowl, footed, 6"	40				160						
Compote	100					200					175 MMG
FILE AND SHELL (SOWERBY)											
Candle Lamp, 9¼"	350										
FILED RIB (FEDERAL)											
Bowl, 8½" – 9"	35										
Bowl, 5"	15										
Plate, 10¾"	65										
FILED STEM											
Vase	75										
FILIGREE (DUGAN)											
Vase, rare		4500									
FINE BLOCK (IMPERIAL)											
Shade			50								
FINE CUT AND ROSES (NORTHWOOD)											
Candy Dish, footed	45	55	70	200		350	325	400	125		
Rose Bowl, footed	125	95	175	400		1000	365		200		175 LV
Candy Dish Variant, footed (no collar base), scarce				100							

Pattern Name	M	A	G	B	PO	AO	IB	IG	W	Red	Other
Rose Bowl Variant, footed, rare (Add 25% for fancy interior)		200	300								500 LV
FINE CUT AND STAR											
Banana Boat, 5"	150										
FINE CUT FLOWERS AND VARIANT (FENTON)											
Compote	65		125								
Goblet	75		125								
FINE CUT HEART (MILLERSBURG)											
Exterior pattern only											
FINE CUT OVALS (MILLERSBURG)											
Exterior pattern only											
FINE CUT RINGS (ENGLISH)											
Bowl, oval	140										
Bowl, round	135										
Butter	170										
Celery	160										
Creamer	145										
Jam Jar w/lid	165										
Stemmed Cake Stand	175										
Stemmed Sugar	145										
Vase	150										
FINE CUT RINGS VARIANT (ENGLISH)											
Cake Stand, footed	200										
Celery Vase	150										
FINE PRISMS AND DIAMONDS (ENGLISH)											
Vase, 7" – 14"											90 AM
FINE RIB (DUGAN)											
Vase, 8" – 15"	60	70	90		125						
FINE RIB (FENTON)											
Vase, 2⅝" base	20	80	90	40	150	700				450	250 SA
Vase, 2⅞" base	35	90	95	125							
FINE RIB (NORTHWOOD)											
Vase, 7" – 14"	25	65	45	165		500	180	195	100		225 AQ
FINE RIB SHADE (ELECTRIC)											
One shape	70										
FIR CONES (FINLAND)											
Pitcher			600								
Tumbler			350								
FIRCONE VASE											
Vase, 11¾", very scarce	600										
FIREFLY (MOTH)-(FINLAND)											
Candlesticks, pair	90										
FIRESTONE TIRE											
Ashtray, advertising, various	100			375							150 AM
FISH BOTTLE											
Novelty Bottle	175										
FISH BOWL											
Bowl, 7½", very scarce	375										
FISHERMAN'S MUG (DUGAN)											
One size	200	125		650	1100						250 HO
FISH HEAD VASE											
Fish Vase, 5½"				500							
FISH NET (DUGAN)											
Epergne		300			350						
FISHSCALES AND BEADS (DUGAN)											
Bowl, 6" – 8"	35	100		300	80				90		
Bride's Basket, complete					150						
Plate, 7"	80	350			75				100		
Plate, Souvenir of Sturgis, Michigan									375		
FISH VASE (JAIN)											
Two sizes, very scarce	125										
FIVE HEARTS (DUGAN)											
Bowl, dome base, 8¼"	125	275			300						
Bowl, flared, very rare	650										
Rose Bowl, rare	1300										
FIVE LILY EPERGNE											
Complete, metal fittings	175	250									
FIVE PANEL											
Candy Jar, stemmed	70										
FIVE PETALS											
Compote, rare	65										90 AM
Bowl, rare		60									
FLANNEL FLOWER (CRYSTAL)											
Cake Stand	140	195									
Compote, large	120	155									
FLARED PANEL											
Shade					75						
FLARED WIDE PANEL											
Atomizer, 3½"	90										
FLASHED DIAMONDS											
Shakers, pair	50										
Vase Whimsey, from creamer	75										

Pattern Name	M	A	G	B	PO	AO	IB	IG	W	Red	Other
FLASHING STARS											
Tumbler, rare		325		275							
Pitcher, rare		950									
FLAT TOP CRUET											
Cruet w/stopper	75										
FLEUR-DE-LIS (INWALD)											
Bowl, 8", rare	350										
Chop Plate, 12", rare	700										
Plate, 6¼", rare	425										
Rose Bowl, rare	525										
Vase, rare	650										
FLEUR-DE-LIS AND VARIANT (MILLERSBURG)											
Bowl, flat, 9" – 10"	225	550	250								6500 V
Bowl, footed, 9" – 10"	225	325	325								
Bowl, footed, square, very rare											5000 V
Bowl, tricornered, scarce	400	650	475								
Compote, very rare			5000								
Rose Bowl, either base, rare		2700									
FLEUR-DE-LIS MINIATURE LAMP											
Mini Gone with the Wind Lamp	375										
FLICKERING FLAMES											
Shade									50		
FLOATING HEN											
Candy w/lid, footed	400										
FLORA (ENGLISH)											
Float Bowl				200							
Vase	100			125							
FLORABELLE											
Pitcher								500			
Tumbler								175			
FLORAL ACCENT											
Cup and Saucer, mini	125										
FLORAL AND GRAPE (DUGAN)											
Hat Whimsey	40										
J.I.P. Whimsey, scarce											100 PHO
Pitcher	145	300		350					325		
Tumbler	20	50		35					55		
FLORAL AND GRAPE (FENTON)											
Pitcher, two variations	195	285	300	300				600			
Tumbler	30	35	100	30							
Pitcher Whimsey Vase, from pitcher, very rare				4500							
FLORAL AND GRAPE VARIANT #2 (FENTON)											
Pitcher				400							
Tumbler				40							
FLORAL AND MELON RIB											
Ale Decanter	600										
Ale Glasses	175										
FLORAL AND OPTIC (IMPERIAL)											
Bowl, footed, 8" – 10"	35				150 MMG					350	140 SM
Cake Plate, footed	60				180 MMG					550	170 SM
Rose Bowl, footed	75				200 MMG						200 AQ
FLORAL AND SCROLL											
Shade, various shapes	45										
FLORAL AND WHEAT (DUGAN)											
Bonbon, stemmed, two shapes	40	125		250	75				125		
FLORAL BUTTERFLIES (FENTON)											
Vase, etched	135										
FLORAL FAN											
Etched Vase	50										
FLORAL OVAL (HIGBEE)											
Bowl, 7"	50										
Creamer	60										
Goblet	75										
Plate, 7", rare	90										
FLORAL SUNBURST (SWEDEN)											
Bowl	95			175							
Rose Bowl	225			325							
Vase, flared top	650			1100							
Vase, tricorner or turned in top	950			1500							
FLORENTINE (FENTON AND NORTHWOOD)											
Candlesticks, large, pair	125		160 RG	700				125		1100	
Candlesticks, small, pair	75		120	450						900	110 CeB
FLORENTINE HAT											
Hat Vase	50										
FLOWER AND DIAMOND											
Jelly Compote	90										
FLOWER BASKET											
One Size	50										
FLOWER BLOCK											
Various Sizes	20+										
FLOWER FROG											
Flower Holder	15	25	30	35			40	40			45 SA

Pattern Name	M	A	G	B	PO	AO	IB	IG	W	Red	Other
FLOWERING DILL (FENTON)											
Hat	25	60	65	50						475	125 IM
FLOWERING VINE (MILLERSBURG)											
Compote, tall, very rare		8500	9500								
FLOWER MEDALLION (INDIANA GLASS)											
Tumbler, rare	400										
FLOWER POT (FENTON)											
One Size, complete	60			75							
FLOWERS AND BEADS (DUGAN)											
Bowl, 6" – 7"	30	60			75						
Plate, six sided, 7½"	75	110			125						
FLOWERS AND FRAMES (DUGAN)											
Bowl, 8" – 10"	60	425			200						
FLOWERS AND SPADES (DUGAN)											
Bowl, 5", scarce		75			65						
Bowl, 9½", rare		350			450						
FLOWER WEB (INDIA)											
Tumbler	175										
FLUFFY PEACOCK (FENTON)											
Pitcher	325	700	750	575							
Tumbler	40	70	110	75							
FLUTE (BRITISH)											
Sherbet, marked "English"	50										
FLUTE (MILLERSBURG)											
Compote, 6" (marked "Kry-stol"), rare	825	2200									
Vase, rare	1100	1250	1500	4500							
FLUTE (NORTHWOOD)											
Bowl, 5"	25	30									
Bowl, 9"	45	55									
Bowl, three in one edge, rare			150								
Butter	135		185								
Celery Vase	75										
Creamer or Sugar	75		95								
Individual Salt, footed	35										
Master Salt, footed	75										50 V
Plate, very scarce	250										150 V
Ring Tree, rare	175										
Rose Bowl, rare	300										
Sherbet	35	50	45								80 TL
Pitcher, rare	375	675	800								
Tumbler, three varieties	50		300								
FLUTE #700 (IMPERIAL)											
Bowl, 5"	30	70									
Bowl, 10"		225									
Celery Vase, rare	275	400									
Chop Plate, 11", rare	350										
Covered Butter	180	240	210								
Creamer or Sugar	90	100	100								
Cruet	90										
Custard Bowl, 11"		300	400								
Fruit Bowl and Base, scarce	300	700	500								900 V
Cup	25	40	40								65 V
Nappy, one handle	60	135									
Pitcher	300	600	500	600							
Tumbler	45	175	150	200						350	300 V
Toothpick, regular	65	110	140	500							300 V
Toothpick, handled	250										
FLUTE #3939 (IMPERIAL)											
Bowl, 5½", rare	60	75	75								
Bowl, 10", rare	80	150	150								
Bowl, Fruit, 11", rare	95	175	175								
Punch Bowl w/base, scarce	300	500	500								
Punch Cup, scarce	35	50	50								
FLUTE AND CANE (IMPERIAL)											
Bowl, 7½" – 10"	30 – 35										
Candlesticks, pair, rare	150										600 SM
Champagne, rare	125										
Compote, large	60										
Milk Pitcher	150										
Pickle Dish	25										
Punch Cup	25										
Pitcher, stemmed, rare	350										400 PM
Tumbler, rare	400										
Wine	60										
FLUTE AND HONEYCOMB (IMPERIAL)											
Bowl, 5", scarce	65	95									60 CM
Bowl, 8½", rare	150										
FLUTED PILLARS											
Exterior pattern only											
FLUTED RIB											
Jelly Jar	50										
FLUTED SCROLLS (DUGAN)											
Rose Bowl, footed, very rare	800	2000									

Pattern Name	M	A	G	B	PO	AO	IB	IG	W	Red	Other
FLUTE FLOWER ARRANGER											
Bowl, scarce	60										
Flower Arranger, pulled from bowl, scarce	75										
FLUTE VARIANT (NORTHWOOD)											
Bowl, 8½"	60		75								
FOLDING FAN (DUGAN)											
Compote	65	75			125						
FOOTED DRAPE (WESTMORELAND)											
Vase	50								50		
FOOTED PRISM PANELS (ENGLISH)											
Vase	85		120	100							
FOOTED SHELL (WESTMORELAND)											
Small, 3"	45	55	60	60	100 MO						75 AM
Large, 5"	40	50	500 GO	55							70 AM
FORGET-ME-NOT (FENTON)											
***BANDED DRAPE STYLE**											
Pitcher	200		350								
Tumbler	35		60								
FORKS											
Cracker Jar, very scarce	1750		600								
FORMAL (DUGAN)											
Hatpin Holder very scarce	900	1100									
Vase, J.I.P., very scarce	600	900									
FORUM (FINLAND)											
Candlesticks, pair											250 PK
FOSTORIA #600 (FOSTORIA)											
Napkin Ring	75										
FOSTORIA #1231 (FOSTORIA)											
Rose Bowl											145 CM
FOSTORIA #1299 (FOSTORIA)											
Tumbler	150										
FOSTORIA'S FLEMISH											
Vase, 8¾"											145 AM
FOUNTAIN (ENGLISH)											
Epergne, silver fittings, various	250										
Lamp, complete, scarce	300										
FOUR FLOWERS (DUGAN)											
Banana Bowl, scarce		400			350						
Bowl, 5" – 7"	35	45			90						
Bowl, 8" – 10"	150	400	500		285						600 V
Plate, 6½"	150	375			175						
Plate, 9" – 10½"	350	2500	375		650						
Rose Bowl, rare	500	900									
Whimsey Bowl					400						
FOUR FLOWERS VARIANT (EUROPEAN)											
Bowl, footed, 8½"		80	125								
Bowl, 9" – 11"	70	75	100		200						225 AM
Bowl on Metal Base, rare		350 LV			300						350 TL
Plate, 10½", rare		450	375								425 TL
FOUR GARLANDS											
Vase, 7½"	225										
FOUR LEAF CLOVER (SOWERBY)											
Bowl, handled, 5"	90										
FOUR PILLARS (NORTHWOOD AND DUGAN)											
Vase	50	60	100			200	225	250			250 SA
FOUR PILLARS WITH DRAPES											
Vase, very scarce	100		325	425							575 SA
FOUR SUITES (JAIN)											
Tumbler	175										
474 (IMPERIAL)											
Bowl, 8" – 9"	45		85								
Compote, 7", rare	125	275									1650 AQ
Cordial, rare	90	210									135 EmG
Goblet	50	90	65								600 LV
Punch Bowl and Base	200	2350	700								600 PK
Punch Cup	15	40	30								
Milk Pitcher, scarce	225	825	375								
Pitcher, standard, scarce	175	3300	500								
Pitcher, large, rare	350	5000									275 VI
Tumbler, scarce	30	100	70	350							
Wine	100										
Vase, 7", rare	375									3200	
Vase, 10", rare	500										
Vase, 14", rare	700		1100								
474 VARIANT (SWEDEN)											
Compote, 7"			125								
49'ER											
Atomizer	90										
Decanter w/stopper	125										
Perfume, three sizes	80										
Pin Box	60										
Pin Tray, two sizes	50										
Powder Box	70										

Pattern Name	M	A	G	B	PO	AO	IB	IG	W	Red	Other
Pitcher, squat	175										
Tumbler	75										
Ring Tray	70										
Wine	80										
49'ER VARIANT (INWALD)											
Decanter, scarce	175										
Tumblers, three sizes, scarce	40 – 125										
Tray, scarce	95										
FOXHUNT											
Decanter	275										
Shot Glass	75										
FRANKLIN FLUTE (U.S. GLASS)											
Hat Whimsey, from tumbler	95										
FREEFOLD (IMPERIAL)											
Vase, 7" – 14"	30	55	45						70		115 SM
FREESIA (FENTON)											
Pitcher	225										
Tumbler	35										
FRENCH GRAPE											
Bowl, 4"	180										
FRENCH KNOTS (FENTON)											
Hat	30	40	40	45							
FRIT PINCHED VASE (DUGAN)											
Vase					150						
FROLICKING BEARS (U.S. GLASS)											
Pitcher, very rare			45000								
Tumbler, very rare			13500								
FRONDS AND ARCHES											
Bowl, 4½"	65										
FROSTED BLOCK (IMPERIAL)											
Bowl, 6½" – 7½"	20										35 CM
Bowl, 9"	30										40 CM
Bowl, square, scarce	35										55 CM
Celery Tray	35										
Compote	40										75 CM
Covered Butter	65										
Creamer or Sugar	30										35 CM
Milk Pitcher, rare	90										
Nut Bowl Whimsey											55 CM
Pickle Dish, handled, rare	70										65 CM
Plate, 7½"	40										65 CM
Plate, 9"	45										150 CM
Rose Bowl	80										100 CM
Vase, 6"	35										100 SM
(Add 10% if marked "Made In USA")											
FROSTED BUTTONS (FENTON)											
Bowl, footed, 10"											175 PM
FROSTED FIRCONE VASE											
Vase, 11¾", rare	800										
FROSTED INDIAN (JAIN)											
Vase	150										
FROSTED LOTUS (INDIA)											
Vase	200										
FROSTED OXFORD											
Bobeche, each	60										
FROSTED RIBBON											
Pitcher	85										
Tumbler	30										
FROSTY											
Bottle	25										
FRUIT AND BERRIES (JENKINS)											
Bean Pot, covered, rare	400			425							
FRUIT BAND											
Decanter	250			350							
Glass	75			90							
FRUIT BASKET (MILLERSBURG)											
Compote, handled, rare		1600									
FRUIT BONBONNIERE											
Bonbonniere w/lid, 5½", very scarce	550										
FRUIT JAR (BALL)											
One Size	50										
FRUIT SALAD											
Punch Bowl and Base, rare	600	700			3900	6000					
Punch Cup, rare	30	40			60						
FRUITS AND FLOWERS (NORTHWOOD)											
Bonbon	65	110	225	175		950	400	675	235		125 VI
Bowl, 7"	30	65	135	145				325			400 AQ
Bowl, 9" – 10½"	65	125	125	250				900	1500		
Plate, 7"	95	125	190	300							
Plate, handgrip, 7", scarce	100	150	200								
Plate, 9½"	115	235									
(*Add 25% for stippled)											
FRUITS AND FLOWERS VARIANT											
Bowl, 7" – 8", very scarce	125		225								

Pattern Name	M	A	G	B	PO	AO	IB	IG	W	Red	Other
FRUITS AND FLUTES											
Bowl	125										
GAELIC (INDIANA GLASS)											
Butter	165										
Creamer or Spooner	60										
Sugar w/lid	85										
GALLOWAY (U.S. GLASS)											
Creamer, small, rare	125										
GANADOR (PAPINI)											
Pitcher	350										
Tumbler	100										
Vase	145										
GANGES GARDEN (INDIA)											
Tumbler	180										
GARDEN ARBOR (INDIA)											
Tumbler	150										
GARDEN MUMS (FENTON)											
Bowl, 5" – 6", scarce		300									
Bowl, 5", deep round, rare		375									
Plate, regular or handgrip, 7"		450									250 LV
GARDEN PATH (DUGAN)											
Bowl, 6" – 7"	35	110			150		1500		100		
Bowl, 8" – 9½", ruffled	75	600			350				350		
Bowl, 10", ice cream shape, scarce	450	1200			950				1000		
Compote, rare	225	400							500		
Plate, 6", rare	425	650			525				425		
Chop Plate, rare	4500	5000			7500						
Rose Bowl, rare	200										
GARDEN PATH VARIANT (DUGAN)											
Bowl, 5¾" – 6½"	40	125			160		1300				
Bowl, 8" – 10", deep round	75	425			300				350		
Chop Plate, rare	4500	5250			7250						
Chop Plate, Soda Gold exterior		6750			7500						
Rose Bowl, rare	200										
GARLAND (FENTON)											
Rose Bowl, footed	45	350	400	90							425 AM
GARLAND AND BOWS (RIIHIMAKE)											
Bowls, various	40 – 75										
Compote	125										
Covered Butter	200										
Creamer	70										
Open Sugar	75										
Salver, low ruffled	225										
GAY 90S (MILLERSBURG)											
Pitcher, rare		8500	9500								
Tumbler, rare	1000	1150	1450								
GEM DANDY BUTTER CHURN											
Butter Churn, complete	500										
GEO. GETZ PIANOS (FENTON)											
Bowl, scarce		1200									
Plate, scarce		1850									
GEORGE (BROCKWITZ)											
Bowl, four sizes	50+										
Compote, three sizes	75+										
Covered Butter	125										
Creamer	65										
Salver	70										
GEORGETTE (INDIA)											
Tumbler	145										
GEORGIA BELLE (DUGAN)											
Card Tray, footed, rare	75	80	95		175						
Compote, footed	65	75	85		140						
GERMAN STEINS											
Various sizes	175+										
GEVURTZ BROTHERS (FENTON)											
Bowl, advertising, scarce		800									
Plate, advertising, rare		2000									
Plate, handgrip, scarce		1400									
GIANT LILY (CZECH)											
Vase	250										
GIBSON GIRL											
Toothpick Holder	60										
GLOBE											
Vase, 9½"	25										
GOA (JAIN)											
Vase, 6½"	300										
GOD AND HOME (DUGAN)											
Pitcher, rare				2200							
Tumbler, rare				175							
GODDESS (JAIN)											
Vase, 8½", rare	750										
GODDESS OF ATHENA											
Epergne, rare			1700								2000 AM
GODDESS OF HARVEST (FENTON)											
Bowl, 9½", very rare	13000	30000		25000							
Plate, very rare		35000									

Pattern Name	M	A	G	B	PO	AO	IB	IG	W	Red	Other
GOLDEN BIRD											
Nappy w/handle, footed	300										
GOLDEN CUPID											
Bowl, 5", rare	225										
GOLDEN FLOWERS											
Vase, 7½"	95										
GOLDEN GRAPES (DUGAN)											
Bowl, 7"	30	40	50								50 CM
Rose Bowl, collar base	90										
GOLDEN HARE (INDIA)											
Pitcher	350										
GOLDEN HARVEST											
Decanter w/stopper	145	250									
Wine	25	35									
GOLDEN HONEYCOMB											
Bowls, various	20 – 35										
Compote	35										
Creamer	25										
Plate	25										
Sugar	40										
GOLDEN OXEN (JEANNETTE)											
Mug	20										
GOLDEN PANSIES											
Tray, 10" x 5½"	350										
GOLDEN PINEAPPLE AND BLACKBERRIES											
Bowl, 9"	400										
Plate, 10"	500										
GOLDEN PRESS											
Wine Bottle, with original label	65										
GOLDEN THISTLE											
Tray, 5", rare	350										
GOLDEN WEDDING											
Bottle, four sizes	20 – 75										
GOLD FISH											
Bowl	125										
GOLIATH											
Vase, 19" – 22", rare	500										
GOOD LUCK (NORTHWOOD)											
Bowl, 8½"	250	400	450	425	3000	2650		14000			1350 SA
Bowl, decorated, very rare				3200							
Proof Bowl, rare	600										
Plate, 9"	450	600	900	1950			9500	20000	11000		1050 HO
(Stippled add 25%)											
GOOD LUCK VARIANT (NORTHWOOD)											
Bowl, 8½", rare	300	425	450								600 LV
Bowl, prototype, 8½", very rare	3250										
Plate, rare	350	375	400								
GOODYEAR											
Ashtray in Tire	225										
GOOSEBERRY SPRAY (U.S. GLASS)											
(Palm Beach exterior)											
Bowl, 5", scarce	75	110									225 HA
Bowl, 5½", tricorner, rare	150								375		225 HA
Bowl, 10", scarce	65	95							200		165 HA
Compote, rare		225							300		
Rose Bowl, 4½", rare	125										325 HA
GOTHIC ARCHES (IMPERIAL)											
Vase, 9" – 17", rare	125										400 SM
GRACE											
Bowl				225							
GRACEFUL (NORTHWOOD)											
Vase	45	85	120	150					200		
GRACEFUL VARIANT (NORTHWOOD)											
Vase (different base)	55	110	145								
GRACEFUL WATER SET											
Pitcher, rare				1500							1700 AM
Tumbler, scarce	450			325							700 AM
GRAND THISTLE (FINLAND)											
Pitcher, rare				700							750 AM
Tumbler, rare				120							350 AM
GRANKVIST (EDA)											
Bowl	165			235							
Rose Bowl	250			375							
GRAPE AND CABLE (FENTON)											
Banana Bowl, flat (two sides up), rare	425										
Bowl, Ball footed, 7" – 8½"	75	90	85	110							130 V
Bowl, flat, 7" – 8"	35	60	80	70	850					750	145 V
Bowl, spatula, footed, 7" – 8"	65	90	95	125							
Bride's Basket, handled, very rare		2000		2600							
Centerpiece Bowl w/Persian Medallion interior, very rare			1500								
Orange Bowl, footed	110	225	250	175							
Orange Bowl, advertising, Pacific Coast Mail Order, rare	2400		3500	2800							

Pattern Name	M	A	G	B	PO	AO	IB	IG	W	Red	Other
Orange Bowl w/Persian Medallion interior, scarce	225	350	600	425				3500			
Plate, spatula, footed, 9"	80	125	175	185						1475	
Spittoon Whimsey, rare	1200										
GRAPE AND CABLE (NORTHWOOD)											
Banana Boat, footed	175	225	350	425		18000	600	500	400		400 PL
Bowl, ruffled, 5½"	25	35	50	75					95		55 LV
Bowl, ruffled, 8" – 9"	45	55	70	95		2750	1000	3000	1000		1500 EmG
Bowl, ruffled, 10" – 11½"	100	140	160	250					525		200 LG
Bowl, spatula footed, 8" – 9"	60	75	100	275				900			
Ice Cream Bowl, 5" – 6"	50	75	175	125				325	100		70 LV
Ice Cream Bowl, 11"	200	450	1250	625				1600	325		350 LV
Bonbon	65	65	175	160					275		385 PL
Breakfast Set, two pieces	150	225	250								
Orange Bowl, footed	175	250	350	450				950	725		4000 MUC
Orange Bowl (Blackberry interior), rare		2200		3000							
Centerpiece Bowl, footed	250	350	900	450			1250	750	550		1500 LG
Candlesticks, each	150	200	250								
Candle lamp, complete	750	800	900								
Compote, covered	2000	350									
Compote, open	300	500	1000								
Cologne w/stopper	160	325	325				550		650		
Cologne Vase Whimsey, very rare		7000									
Cup and Saucer, rare	400	450									
Dresser Tray	165	275	300				900		1000		
Fernery, scarce	1000	1300	1600				1800	3500	1000		700 IC
Hatpin Holder	200	300	350	1200		13500	2300	1450	2500		600 EmG
Hatpin Whimsey Vase, rare		4300	5200								
Nappy (from punch cup)	50	75	75	100			625				
Oil Lamp Whimsey		3500									
Powder Jar w/lid	135	175	250	475		4000	700	1650	1750		550 LV
Pin Tray	125	250	300				700		800		400 IC
Plate, spatula footed, 9"	65	100	125	550				500			
Plate, flat, 7" – 7½"	800	175	225								275 HO
Plate, flat, 8" – 9"	165	225	275	750			2800				2700 SA
Plate, handgrip	150	200	225								400 HO
Plate, two sides up	150	175	350								
Plate, advertising			575								
Punch Bowl and Base, small	300	600	700	1500		120000	9000	8000	4500		
Punch Bowl and Base, mid-size	375	750	800	1800			20000	18000	5000		
Punch Bowl and Base, banquet	2000	2200	3100	4300			60000	65000	9000		
Punch Cup, two sizes	25	30	40	60		1200	100	125	70		
Shade	175	200									
Spittoon, from powder jar, very rare	5000	6500	6000								
Sweetmeat w/lid	2800	200		3000							
Sweetmeat Whimsey Compote	400	300									
*(Stippled pieces, add 25%)											
*(Pie crust edge bowls and plates, add 10%)											
GRAPE AND CABLE BANDED (NORTHWOOD)											
Banana Bowl	275			600							650 ReB
Dresser Tray	135										
Hatpin Holder	250	450		700							
Orange Bowl	425			650							3000 IC
GRAPE AND CABLE VARIANT (NORTHWOOD)											
Bowl, 6" – 8"	65	75	90	145		3900	900				325 EmG
Plate, 7½" – 9", scarce	135	250	650	550							1200 EmG
Plate, handgrip, scarce	165	190	245	500							325 LV
Plate, two sides up, 6" – 7½", scarce	125	200									
(Stippled pieces, add 25%)											
GRAPE AND CABLE WITH THUMBPRINT (NORTHWOOD)											
Berry Bowl, 5½"	20	40	50	125				100			
Berry Bowl, 9" – 10"	90	145	175					375			
Butter	150	225	225				2300				
Cracker Jar	300	450		600		15000		2500	1200		
Creamer	65	80	95				550				
Decanter w/stopper	600	700									
Hat Whimsey, from tumbler	75	125	125								150 AM
Pitcher, regular	200	275	325					8000			800 SM
Pitcher, tankard	475	800	2500					6500			1000 LV
Sherbet	35	45	60								
Tumbler, regular	25	35	45					500			
Tumbler, tankard	50	60	75					525			
Tobacco Jar (humidor)	300	475		650							600 SM
Shot Glass	115	195									
Spittoon, from humidor, very rare	7500										
Spooner	60	70	85				625				
Sugar	70	95	140				900				
*Stippled pieces add 25%											
GRAPE AND CHERRY (ENGLISH)											
Bowl, 8½", rare	100			200							

Pattern Name	M	A	G	B	PO	AO	IB	IG	W	Red	Other
GRAPE AND GOTHIC ARCHES (NORTHWOOD)											
Bowl, 5"	15	40	40	50							225 AQ
Bowl, 10"	70	95	100	200							150 PL
Butter	100	150	150	150							425 PL
Creamer or Spooner	40	85	85	70							125 PL
Sugar w/lid	75	100	100	125							125 PL
Pitcher	300	395	425	475							750 PL
Tumbler	30	80	110	75							175 PL
GRAPE ARBOR (DUGAN)											
(Feather Scroll exterior)											
Bowl, footed, 9½" – 11"	150	300		500	1200				150		
GRAPE ARBOR (NORTHWOOD)											
Hat	60	100		145			225	325	110		
Pitcher	325	625	14000				1300	10000	425		
Tumbler	45	100		400			160	325	70		
Tumbler (etched)		450		575					75		140 LV
GRAPE BASKET											
Basket, handled	55		85	225							
GRAPE DELIGHT (DUGAN)											
Nut Bowl, footed, 6"	50	120		80					95		
Rose Bowl, footed, 6"	65	125		100					65		
GRAPE FRIEZE (NORTHWOOD)											
Bowl, 10½", rare											800 IC
GRAPE LEAVES (MILLERSBURG)											
Bowl, 9", very scarce	600	800	900								3000 V
Bowl, 7" – 8", square, very rare		3200	5000								
Bowl, 7" – 8", tricorner, very rare			4200								
GRAPE LEAVES (NORTHWOOD)											
Bowl, 8½", ruffled or three in one edge	45	95	85	150			1400				225 AM
Bride's Basket, complete		300									
GRAPES OF RATH											
Vase, 6⅝", very scarce	225										
GRAPE SPITTOON											
Spittoon, one shape, rare	1500										
GRAPE VARIANT											
Tumbler Variant	30	55	35						125		
GRAPEVINE AND SPIKES (JAIN)											
Tumbler	250										
GRAPEVINE LATTICE (DUGAN)											
Bowl, 6" – 7"	30	65							50		75 LV
Hat shape, J.I.P.	75	150									
Plate, 6½" – 7½"	145	200		325					150		375 LV
Pitcher, rare	325	850		1200					950		
Tumbler, rare	50	75		165					150		
GRAPE WREATH (MILLERSBURG)											
Bowl, 5"	95	120	165								
Bowl, 7½" – 9"	100	125	150	800							
Bowl, ice cream, 10"	400	275	300								
Spittoon Whimsey, rare	3500		4000								
GRAPE WREATH CLOVER AND FEATHER VARIANT											
Bowl, 5½"	75	125	100								
Bowl, 5½", tricorner			275								
Bowl, 7" – 9"	100	150	175								
GRAPE WREATH/MULTI-STAR VARIANT (MILLERSBURG)											
Bowl, 5"	50	60	70								
Bowl, 7½"	70	80	90								
Bowl, 9"	90	90	90								
Bowl, ice cream, 10"	150	175	175								
GRAPE WREATH VARIANT (MILLERSBURG)											
Bowl, 5"	40	65	70								
Bowl, 7½"	50	75	80								
Bowl, 9"	55	90	100								
Bowl, ice cream, 10"	125	150	150								
GRECIAN DAISY											
Pitcher, scarce	400										
Tumbler, scarce	60										
GRECIAN SPITTOON											
Spittoon, with reticulated edge	250										
GRECIAN URN											
Perfume, 6"	50										
GREEK KEY (NORTHWOOD)											
Bowl, 7" – 8½", collar base	150	200	225	400				2700			
Plate, 9", scarce (basketweave back)	1250	700	850	2000							
Plate w/rib back, 9", rare	3850										
Pitcher, rare	750	900	1800								
Tumbler, rare	110	225	235								
GREEK KEY AND LEAF LAMP											
Lamp, very scarce	400										
GREEK KEY AND SCALES (NORTHWOOD)											
Bowl, dome footed	75	100	100				1500				

Pattern Name	M	A	G	B	PO	AO	IB	IG	W	Red	Other
GREENGARD FURNITURE (MILLERSBURG)											
Bowl, advertising, very rare		1900									
Plate, handgrip, rare		2200									
GROUND CHERRIES											
Pitcher				125							
Tumbler				50							
GUEST SET (FENTON)											
Pitcher and Tumble-up, complete	200										
GUM TIPS VASE (CRYSTAL)											
Vase (eight ribs), very scarce		375									400 BA
GUM TIPS VASE VARIANT (CRYSTAL)											
Vase (ten ribs), very scarce		400									450 BA
HAIR RECEIVER											
Complete	75										
HALF SHOT MINIATURE											
Miniature Shot Glass	35										
HALLOWEEN											
Pitcher, two sizes	375										
Tumbler, two sizes	50										
Spittoon	600										
HAMBURG (SWEDEN)											
Jardiniere				225							
HAMILTON SOUVENIR											
Vase, 6¼"	70										
HAMMERED BELL CHANDELIER											
Complete, five shades									600		
Shade, each									75		
HANDLED CANDLEHOLDER											
Candlestick, with handle	100										
HANDLED TUMBLER											
One size	75	125									
HANDLED VASE (IMPERIAL)											
Three shapes	45										90 SM
Candle Bowl, scarce	110	500									
HAND VASE (JAIN)											
One shape, 5½" – 8"	90	450								1450	
HAPPY PUP											
Novelty	75										
HARVARD YARD											
Decanter w/stopper, 11½"	250										
HARVEST FLOWER (DIAMOND)											
Pitcher, rare	2800										
Tumbler, very scarce – rare	200	900	1100								
HARVEST POPPY											
Compote, scarce	320	450	400	450							500 AM
HATCHET (U.S. GLASS)											
One shape	175										
HATPINS (VARIOUS MAKERS) (ALL PATTERNS LISTED BELOW)											
Banded Basketweave		90									
Banded Berry Cluster											135 LV
Basket Flower		75									
Banded Criss Cross		85									
Banded Flower											100 LV
Bars and Beads		120									
Beaded Ball Bat		45									
Beaded oval		75									
Beaded Fringe		175									
Beaded Parasol		75									
Beaded Pinwheel		400									
Beaded Tears		225									
Bee on Flower		600									
Bee on Honeycomb											135 AM
Beetle		115									
Belle		225									
Big Butterfly		80									
Bird of Paradise		1100									
Blister Beetle				1500							
Bordered Cosmos		125									125 BA
Border Path		37									
Bubbles		200									
Bullet		125									
Bumblebee (Dragonfly)		60									
Butlers Mirror		50									
Butterfly		100									
Button and Fan		60									
Cameo		200									
Cane		200									
Checkers		200									
Cherries		115									
Christmas Star		300									
Circled Basketweave		145									
Cockatoo		800									
Concentric Circles											200 LV
Coolie Hat		45									

Pattern Name	M	A	G	B	PO	AO	IB	IG	W	Red	Other
Coqui		1800									
Corona		165									
Daisy and Button		100									
Diamond Spearhead	145	300									
Diamond Sphere		375									
Diamond and oval		300									
Dimples		135									
Dimples and Brilliance		225									
Dinner Ring		250									
Dogwood		200									
Dots and Curves		50									
Double Crown		55									
Doves		350									
Dragonflies		65									
Elegance		120									
Elegance Variant		160									
Embroidered Circles		150									
Faceted Butterfly		150									
Faceted Dome		85									
Faceted ovals		75									
Faceted Spearhead		150									
Faceted Dome		175									
Fancy Beetle		400									
Ferris Wheel		400									
Floral Spray		165									65 AM
Flower Arcs		85									
Flower Petals		325									
Flying Bat	100	135	200								200 BA
Four Hearts (Hearts and Cross)		300									
Fringed Beads		250									
Fuschia Basket		2100	2250								
Gazebo		700									
Geisha Girl		800									
Grape		750	800	800							300 LV
Greek Key Variant		75									
Hearts and Cross (Four Hearts)		65									
Honeycomb Ornament		80		125							
Horsefly		250									
Indian blanket			300								
Iridized Star			225								
Isabelle		1800									
Japanese Garden		600									
Jute Braid		225									
King Spider		700									
Knotty Tree Bark			900	900							900 LV
Large Beetle		800									
Laurel Jewel		325									
Leaf Beetle			1200								
Leaf and Veil		400									
Long Prisms		75									
Looped Buckle		200									
Lots of Diamonds		150									
Marquisite Flower (Anemome Cushion)		250									
Marvelous		550									
Moire Beetle		40									
Nasty Bug		1800									
Nautical											250 CM
Orchid (Flower and Jewel)		700									
Oval Prisms		75									
Oval Sphere		75									
Owl, two sizes	2000		1000								900 LV
Owl, Horned		1400									
Paisley		50									
Peacock		2000	2000	3000			2000				
Penstar		175									
Piazza		350									
Pine Sawyer			800								
Pith Helmet		500					600				500 Brown
Prisms		75									
Propeller		600									
Propeller Variant		625									
Rectangular Diamonds		175									
Ribbon Triangle		475									
Rooster		150	100	65			110			115	60 AQ
Royal Scarab										350	
Salamanders		75									
Scarab		100									150 AM
Scarab Shell		450	500								1050 LV
Shell			600								
Shining Peaks and Valleys		700									
Six Plums		55									
Snake Head		300									
Spider	250										125 AM
Spinner											225 MMG
Spiral Dance		80									

Pattern Name	M	A	G	B	PO	AO	IB	IG	W	Red	Other
Spring Buds											500 SM
Star Center		100									
Star Prism		400									
Star and Flower				1100							
Star and Diamond Point		75									
Star and Nearcut		60									
Star and Rosette		75									
Star and Scroll		85									
Star of David and Baguetted		500									
Stork				2800							
Strawberry			1000								1100 AM
Stubby Beetle			700								
Stylized Scarab		175	200								
Sunflower									75		
Suns Up		200									220 LV
Swirley Taffeta		175									
Throw Pillow		75									
Tiny Triangle Back Beetle											700 BA
Top of the Morning		200									
Top of the Walk		200									
Triad		60									
Triangle Back Beetle		500	700								
Triplets		55									
True Scarab				825							
Tufted Throw Pillow		45									
Turban		85									
Twin Gators		1300									
Two Flowers		150									
Two Flowers Variant				250							
Ugly Bug		1600									
Umbrella Prisms, small		50									
Umbrella Prisms, large		75									
Veiling		50									
Vintage Cluster											350 SM
Waves		100	125	160							225 ICG
Wavy Satin		95									
Whirling Cobblestones		400									
Zig Zag											125 AM
HATTIE (IMPERIAL)											
Bowl	60	295	135	725							150 SM
Plate, very scarce	2000	2800	600								3500 AM
Rose Bowl	600	3000									1500 AM
HAVELLI (INDIA)											
Tumbler	180										
HAWAIIAN LEI (HIGBEE)											
Sugar	75										
Creamer	75										
HAWAIIAN MOON											
Pitcher	200										250 CRAN
Tumbler	75										90 CRAN
HAZEL											
Vase, scarce	225										
HEADDRESS											
Bowl, 7" – 10"	175			225							
Compote	80			125							
HEADDRESS VARIANT (COSMOS AND CANE EXTERIOR)											
Bowl, 7" – 10"	125		200	175					195		145 HA
HEART AND HORSESHOE (FENTON)											
Bowl, 8½"	2500										
Plate, 9", rare	4000							18000			
HEART AND TREES (FENTON)											
Bowl, 8¼"	350		700								
HEART AND VINE (FENTON)											
Bowl, 8½"	60	75	95	85							125 LV
Plate, 9", very scarce		400	625	900							
Plate, advertising (Spectors), rare	1600										
HEART AND VINE VARIANT (FENTON)											
Plate, 9", scarce	800			1000							
HEART BAND											
One Shape (salt)	45										
HEART BAND SOUVENIR (MCKEE)											
Mug, small	55		100								125 AQ
Mug, large	70		125								150 AQ
Tumbler, mini or shot glass	35		70								
Tumbler, rare	250		325								450 LV
HEART HANDLE DOUBLE SALT											
Double Salt with center handle, rare	250										
HEARTS AND FLOWERS (NORTHWOOD)											
Banana Bowl Whimsey, very rare		850									
Bowl, 8½", ruffled	325	425	1800	850		6500	600	800	300		2300 EmG
Bowl, 8½", pie crust edge	550	625	1300	2800		6500	625	1600	450		
Compote	200	350	1500	325		600	700	850	175		600 LV
Plate, 9", scarce	1100	1500	2000	6500			1900	2800	3200		25000 V

Pattern Name	M	A	G	B	PO	AO	IB	IG	W	Red	Other
HEART SWIRL											
Lamp	450										
HEAVY BANDED DIAMONDS (CRYSTAL)											
Bowl, 5"	50	75									
Bowl, 9"	100	125									
Flower Set, two pieces	150	195									
Pitcher, very scarce	900	1250									
Tumbler, very scarce	250	400									
HEAVY DIAMOND											
Nappy	40										
HEAVY DIAMOND (IMPERIAL)											
Bowl, 10"	45										
Compote	45		55								
Creamer	30										
Sugar	35										
Vase	50		65								85 SM
HEAVY DRAPE (FOSTORIA)											
Vase, 7½"	90										
HEAVY GRAPE (DUGAN)											
Bowl, 5", scarce	125	175			225						
Bowl, 10", scarce	700	550			435						
HEAVY GRAPE (IMPERIAL)											
Bowl, 5" – 6"	25	40	30	500							70 AM
Bowl, 7" – 8"	35	55	45								125 SM
Bowl, 9" – 10"	100	250	165	800							300 AM
Fruit Bowl w/base	275										400 AM
Nappy	45	55	50								75 OG
Plate, 6"	300										
Plate, 8"	65	200	200								225 SM
Plate, 11"	225	850	300						450		400 AM
Punch Bowl w/base	350	950	525								1000 AM
Punch Cup	55	100	75								85 AM
HEAVY HEART (HIGBEE)											
Tumbler	150										
HEAVY HOBNAIL (FENTON)											
Vase, rare		600							475		
HEAVY HOBS											
Lamp (amber base glass)					300						
HEAVY IRIS (DUGAN)											
Pitcher	250	1000			2500				1100		
Tumbler	60	105							175		125 HO
Tumbler Whimsey	350								400		
HEAVY PINEAPPLE (FENTON)											
Bowl, flat or footed, 10"	1000			1500					2000		1600 AM
HEAVY PRISMS (ENGLISH)											
Celery Vase, 6"	85	115		100							
HEAVY SHELL											
Bowl, 8¼"									150		
Candleholder, each									100		
HEAVY VINE											
Atomizer	85										
Cologne	90										
Lamp	250										
Powder Box	75										
Tumbler	150										
Tumble-up	200										
Shot Glass	80										
HEAVY WEB (DUGAN)											
Bowl, 10", very scarce					700						
Plate, 11", rare					3500						
HEINZ											
Bottle											60 CM
HEINZ TOMATO JUICE											
Juice Glass	75										
HEISEY CARTWHEEL											
Compote											85 PM
HEISEY #352											
Jar with lid	100										
HEISEY #357											
Tumbler, scarce	85										
Water Bottle	190										
HEISEY #473 (NARROW FLUTE WITH RIM)											
Creamer and Tray	150										
HEISEY COLONIAL											
Compote	80										150 Y
Dresser Tray	100										
Hair Receiver	135										
Juice Tumbler	65										
Perfume (cologne)	90										
Puff Box	120										
Vase	75										
HEISEY CRYSTOLITE (HEISEY)											
Spittoon	150										

Pattern Name	M	A	G	B	PO	AO	IB	IG	W	Red	Other
HEISEY FLORAL SPRAY											
Stemmed Candy w/lid, 11"							100				
HEISEY FLUTE											
Punch Cup	35										
Toothpick Holder	150										
HEISEY LAVERNE (HEISEY)											
Bowl, footed, 11", rare	300										
HEISEY OLD WILLIAMSBURG											
Candlestick w/prisms	350										
HEISEY PURITAN (#341)											
Compote	75	200									150 V
Compote, tricorner whimsey	125										
HELEN'S STAR (INDIA)											
Vase	190										
HELIO											
Vase, 5" – 6", very rare	200										
HERON (DUGAN)											
Mug, rare	1500	125									
HERRINGBONE AND BEADED OVALS											
Compote, rare	200										
HERRINGBONE AND MUMS (JEANNETTE)											
Tumbler, very rare	400										
HEXAGON AND CANE (IMPERIAL)											
Covered Sugar	90										
HEXAGON SQUARE											
Child's Breakfast Set (complete)											60 LV
HEX BASE											
Candlesticks, pair	75	125	110								175 SM
HEX OPTIC (HONEYCOMB) (JEANNETTE-DEPRESSION ERA)											
Bonbon	20										
Bowl, 5"	10										
Compote	25										
Creamer or Sugar	20										
Lamp, Oil	100										
Lamp Shade	80										
Plate, 7"	25										
Pitcher	125										
Tumbler	25										
HEX PANEL (JEANNETTE)											
Parfait or Soda	60										
HICKMAN											
Banana Bowl Whimsey, very rare	150										
Caster Set, four pieces	325										450 PM
Rose Bowl, rare	200										
HIGBEE ADVERTISING MUG											
Miniature Advertising Mug, rare	200										
HOBNAIL (FENTON)											
Vase, 5" – 11"									100		
HOBNAIL (MILLERSBURG)											
Butter, rare	450	325	650	1000							
Creamer or Spooner, rare	275	375	450	625							
Sugar w/lid, rare	350	500	575	750							
Hat Whimsey, rare	1700										
Pitcher, rare	3000	2500	4000	5000							
Tumbler, rare	1700	750	1500	1100							
Rose Bowl, scarce	225	350	1300								
Spittoon, scarce	700	625	1800								
HOBNAIL AND CANE (CRYSTAL)											
Compote	85	165					225				
Salver	100	190					250				
HOBNAIL PANELS (MCKEE)											
Vase, 8¼"											70 CM
HOBNAIL SODA GOLD											
Spittoon, large	65		100								125 AM
HOBNAIL VARIANT (MILLERSBURG)											
Jardiniere, rare		950		1500							
Rose Bowl, rare	800										
Vase Whimsey, rare	600	700	800								
Salver	100	190					250				
HOBSTAR (IMPERIAL)											
Bowl, Berry, 5"	25										15 CM
Bowl, Berry, 10"	40										30 CM
Bowls, various shapes, 6" – 12"	30										40 CM
Bride's Basket, complete	75										
Butter	80	195	185								90 CM
Cookie Jar w/lid	65		100								
Creamer or Spooner	45	85	75								50 CM
Fruit Bowl w/base	100	250	150								
Pickle Castor, complete	750										
Sugar w/lid	65	100	90								60 CM
Vase, flared	350	200									
HOBSTAR AND ARCHES (IMPERIAL)											
Bowl, 4½"	20	40	25								
Bowl, 9"	55	75	60								60 SM

Pattern Name	M	A	G	B	PO	AO	IB	IG	W	Red	Other
Fruit Bowl w/base	125	300	225								
HOBSTAR AND CUT TRIANGLES (ENGLISH)											
Bowl	30	40	60								
Plate	70	100	110								
Rose Bowl	45	55	70								
HOBSTAR DIAMONDS											
Tumbler, very rare	500										
HOBSTAR AND FEATHER (MILLERSBURG)											
Bowl, round or square, 5", rare		625	1400								
Bowl, 6" – 9", square, rare	750										
Bowl, 6", tricorner, rare									900		
Bridge Piece, diamond, 5", rare	800										
Bridge Piece, heart, 5", rare	775										
Butter, rare	1500	1800	1900								
Card Tray Whimsey, very rare									750		
Compote, 6", rare	1250										
Compote Whimsey (from rose bowl), rare		7000	8000								
Creamer, rare	750	900	1100								
Dessert, stemmed, rare	650	700									
Punch Bowl and Base (flared), very scarce	1400	2800									
Punch Bowl and Base (tulip top), rare	2200	7500									
(*On Punch Bowl and Base, add 25% for Fleur-De-Lis interior)											
Punch Cup, scarce	40	50	65	950							
Punch Bowl Whimsey, rare			7200								
Rose Bowl, giant, rare	9000	3000	1400								
Spittoon Whimsey, very rare		6500									
Spooner, rare		825	1200								4000 V
Stemmed Whimsey Tray, footed, 4½", very rare	800										
Sugar, w/lid, rare		950	1250								4250 V
Tricorner Whimsey, very rare									750		
Vase Whimsey, rare		12000	8000								
HOBSTAR AND FILE											
Pitcher, rare	1700										
Tumbler, rare	200										
HOBSTAR AND FRUIT (WESTMORELAND)											
Bowl, 6", rare					115	300					350 MMG
Plate, 10½", rare							385				
HOBSTAR AND SHIELD (EUROPEAN)											
Pitcher	325										
Tumbler	125										
HOBSTAR AND TASSELS (IMPERIAL)											
Bowl, 6", deep round, rare	125	175	225								
Bowl, 7" – 8", scarce	150	200									350 TL
Plate, 7½", rare			900*								
HOBSTAR AND WAFFLE BLOCK (IMPERIAL)											
Basket	100										
HOBSTAR BAND											
Bowl, 8" – 10", rare	75										
Butter, scarce	200	275									
Celery, scarce	70		225								
Compote, scarce	90										
Pitcher, two shapes, scarce	250										
Tumbler, two shapes	35										
Sugar w/lid	115										
Spooner	65										
HOBSTAR DIAMONDS											
Tumbler, rare	150										
HOBSTAR FLOWER (IMPERIAL)											
Compote, very scarce	60	110	110								200 SM
Cruet, rare	400										
HOBSTAR NU-CUT											
Vase	150	200									500 AM
HOBSTAR PANELS (ENGLISH)											
Creamer	45										
Sugar, stemmed	45										
HOBSTAR REVERSED (ENGLISH)											
Butter	55	75		70							
Frog and Holder	85										
Rose Bowl	60	95									
Spooner	45										
HOCKING FLUTE											
Tumbler	100										
HOCKING MIXING BOWL											
Four sizes (nesting set)	30+										
HOFFMAN HOUSE (IMPERIAL)											
Goblet, very scarce										350	150 AM

Pattern Name	M	A	G	B	PO	AO	IB	IG	W	Red	Other
HOLIDAY											
Bottle											75 PM
HOLIDAY (NORTHWOOD)											
Tray, 11", scarce	225										
HOLLOW TUBE CANDLESTICKS											
Candeholder with prisms, each	35										
HOLLY (FENTON)											
Bowl, 8" – 10"	40	70	80	75					140	900	155 AM
Bowl, deep, 7½"	60			90						1200	150 BA
Compote, 5"	25	100	125	45					750	800	110 PB
Goblet	30	110	200	80						750	100 TL
Hat	20			55		900				300	125 IM
Plate, 9"	300	550	675	425		19000			225	4000	175 CM
Rose Bowl, very scarce	250			325							650 V
HOLLY AND BERRY (DUGAN)											
Bowl, 6" – 7½"	55	110			90						
Nappy	70	125		325	90						225 PKA
HOLLY AND POINSETTIA (DUGAN)											
Compote, very rare	5000										
HOLLY SPRIG (MILLERSBURG)											
Bonbon, two shapes,	50	75	80								100 LV
Bowl, 5½", deep sauce, rare	325	225	300								
Bowl, 5½" – 6", ice cream or three in one shape, very scarce	325	350	375								
Bowl, 5½" – 6", ruffled or candy ribbon edge, scarce	250	225	300								
Bowl, 7" – 8", ruffled, deep, ice cream or candy ribbon edge	250	275	325								
Bowl, 7" – 8", tricorner	275	300	325								
Bowl, 7" – 8", square, scarce	325	350	400								
Bowl, round or ruffled, 9" – 10"	120	175	225								75 CM
Bowl, tricorner, 9" – 10"	325	400	500								
Compote, rare	900	1250	2100								1500 V
Nappy, tricornered	80	95	100								1600 V
Rose Bowl Whimsey, rare	500										2800 V
HOLLY WHIRL (MILLERSBURG)											
Bonbon, two shapes	60	80	85								
Bonbon (Isaac Benesch)	140										
Bowl, 9" – 10", round or ruffled	125	185	235								
Bowl, large, tricorner	350	425	525								
Nappy, tricornered	85	95	110								
HOLLY WREATH (MILLERSBURG)											
Bowl, 6", candy ribbon edge, very scarce	225	350	375								
Bowl, 7½" – 9", ruffled or three in one	175	325	350								
Bowl, 8" – 9", ice cream shape	200	350	375								
(All have four feather center)											
HOLLY WREATH VARIANTS (MILLERSBURG)											
Bowl, 6", candy ribbon edge, very scarce	225	350	375								
Bowl, 7½" – 9", ruffled or three in one	175	325	350								
Bowl, 8" – 9", ice cream shape	200	350	375								
(*These have Multi-Star, Clover, or Sunburst Centers.)											
HOLM SPRAY											
Atomizer, 3"	65										
HOMESTEAD LAMP											
Painted Electric Lamp	175										
HOMESTEAD PENNA.											
Shade									100		
HOMESTEAD SHADE											
Shade	45										
HONEYBEE (JEANNETTE)											
Honey Pot w/lid				180							85 TL
HONEYCOMB (DUGAN)											
Rose Bowl	75				125						
Rose Bowl (pontil base)	150										
HONEYCOMB AND CLOVER (FENTON)											
Bonbon	30	50	50	40							90 V
Compote	35	50	60	50							
Spooner, rare	100										200 AM
HONEYCOMB AND HOBSTAR (MILLERSBURG)											
Vase, 8¼", rare		7300		8200							
HONEYCOMB PANELS											
Tumbler		175									
HONEYCOMB VARIANT (DUGAN)											
Banana Bowl, scarce				90							
Bowl, 6" – 7½"	35	55		65							
Plate, 7" – 7½"	45	95		75							
HOOPS											
Bowl, 8", scarce	50										
Rose Bowl, low, 6½"	75										
HORN OF PLENTY											
Bottle	50										
HORSE CHESTNUT (FENTON)											
Exterior pattern only											

Pattern Name	M	A	G	B	PO	AO	IB	IG	W	Red	Other
HORSES' HEAD (FENTON) (HORSE MEDALLION)											
Bowl, flat, 7½"	200	500	275	220						1250	850 AB
Bowl, footed, 7" – 8"	100	225	325	225						1600	350 TL
Nut Bowl, scarce	80	250		300						1300	500 V
Plate, 6½" – 8½"	300	3250	4000	850							1500 PB
Rose Bowl, footed	165		1300	350						6000	725 V
HORSE RADISH											
Jar w/lid	55										
HORSESHOE											
Shot Glass	35										
HOT SPRINGS SOUVENIR											
Vase, 9⅞", rare	100										
HOURGLASS											
Bud Vase	45										
HOWARD ADVERTISING (FOUR PILLARS) (NORTHWOOD)											
Vase			125								
HUACO DE ORO											
Bottle	175										
HUMPTY-DUMPTY											
Mustard Jar	75										
HYACINTH GONE WITH THE WIND LAMP											
Lamp, rare											4000 CA
ICEBURG (CZECH)											
Bowl							95				
ICE CRYSTALS											
Bowl, footed									85		
Candlesticks, pair									160		
Plate									150		
Salt, footed									65		
IDYLL (FENTON)											
Vase, very rare	650	800		900							
ILLINOIS DAISY (ENGLISH)											
Bowl, 8"	40										
Cookie Jar w/lid	60										
ILLINOIS SOLDIERS AND SAILORS (FENTON)											
Plate (Illinois), scarce	2100	3500		1900							
ILLUSION (FENTON)											
Bonbon	45			75							
IMPERIAL (ARGENTINA)											
Pitcher, very scarce	400										
IMPERIAL #5											
Bowl, 8"		50									65 AM
Vase, 6", rare		175									
IMPERIAL #30 CUT											
Fruit Bowl, 9", handled	75										125 SM
Tray, 10", handled	65										100 SM
IMPERIAL #107½											
Compote or Goblet	40	65									80 TL
IMPERIAL #107½A											
Compote or Goblet	40	65									90 AM
IMPERIAL #203A											
Mug	65										
IMPERIAL #284											
Vase, 6" – 14"	100	225	160								
IMPERIAL #302											
Cruet w/stopper, scarce	400										
IMPERIAL # 393½											
Pitcher	250										
Tumbler	65										
IMPERIAL #499											
Sherbet	15		30							95	
IMPERIAL #537											
Compote	175										
IMPERIAL #641											
Cheese Compote	25										40 SM
Cheese Plate	50										100 SM
IMPERIAL #664											
Tray, center handle											65 SM
IMPERIAL #3937C											
Berry Bowl, small	20		25	150							
Berry Bowl, large	50		60								
IMPERIAL BASKET											
One Shape, rare	150										175 SM
IMPERIAL DAISY											
Shade	45										
IMPERIAL FLUTE VASE											
Vase w/serrated top	40	80	65	500							
IMPERIAL GRAPE											
Basket, handled	55		85	225							75 SM
Bowl, 5"	15	40	30								75 OG
Bowl, 8" – 9", low ruffled	60	260	65	2300	1600						
Bowl, 10" – 11", flared	65	375	75								200 SM

Pattern Name	M	A	G	B	PO	AO	IB	IG	W	Red	Other
Bowl, 10" – 12", ruffled	65	175	100	900							225 SM
Bowl, ice cream shape, scarce	200	400									
Compote	150	190	75								200 AQ
Cup and Saucer	75	175	95								
Decanter w/stopper	95	325	125								300 SM
Goblet	30	100	45								75 AM
Nappy	25		40								35 SM
Milk Pitcher	225	350	200								225 SM
Plate, 6½"	125	295	100	3500							250 LV
Plate, 9"	100	2500	100								1100 AM
Pitcher	100	500	150								325 SM
Tumbler	20	55	90								75 SM
Tumbler Variant	30	55	35								225 W
Punch Bowl and Base	150	450	275								375 SM
Punch Cup	20	45	30								35 SM
Rose Bowl, rare	450	900	300								650 AM
Shade	85										
Spittoon Whimsey, rare	2200		2750								
Water Bottle, scarce	200	185	150								175 LV
Wine	25	75	35								95 SM
IMPERIAL GRAPE VARIANT											
Bowl, 8", scarce	65										
IMPERIAL GRAPE VARIANT #2											
Shallow Bowl, 6½", very scarce	80										
IMPERIAL GRECIAN											
Compote, handled	65										
IMPERIAL JEWELS											
Bowl, 4" – 6"		45	35	55						100	
Bowl, 7" – 10"		60	45	70						150	
Creamer or Sugar										200	70 CeB
Hat shape		70								225	100 CeB
Plate, 7"		75	60	80						225	
Vase, 5" – 12"	100	100	80	110						250	300 AB
IMPERIAL PAPERWEIGHT											
Advertising Paperweight, very rare		1200									
IMPERIAL QUILTED FLUTE											
*Exterior pattern only of Heavy Grape											
IMPERIAL TUBE VASE											
Vase, 5½"											75 EmG
IMPERIAL VINTAGE											
Tray, center handled	35										60 SM
IMPERIAL WIDE RAYS											
Bowl, 9"	30								35		35 CM
Bowl, square, 8", scarce	40								45		40 CM
INCA BOTTLE (ARGENTINA)											
Bottle, scarce	175										
INCA SUN BOTTLE (ARGENTINA)											
Bottle, scarce	200										
INCA VASE											
Vase, very scarce	850										
INCA VASE VARIANT											
Vase, very scarce	950										
INDIA DAISY (INDIA)											
Tumbler	100										
INDIANA FLUTE											
Compote	70										
Rose Bowl, 4½" – 5", very scarce	100										
INDIANA GOBLET (INDIANA GLASS)											
One Shape, rare											800 AM
INDIANA SOLDIERS AND SAILORS (FENTON)											
Bowl, very rare				25000							
Plate, very rare				28000							
INDIANA STATEHOUSE (FENTON)											
Plate, rare	20000			16000							
INDIAN BANGLES (INDIA)											
Pitcher	325										
Tumbler	125										
INDIAN BRACELET (INDIA)											
Pitcher	350										
Tumbler	100										
INDIAN CANOE											
Novelty Canoe Shape	85										
INDIAN CANOE #2											
Novelty Canoe, rope biding on sides	100										
INDIAN ENAMELED BLOSSOMS (INDIA)											
Tumbler	125										
INDIA KEY (INDIA)											
Tumbler	135										
INDIAN WATER JARS (KALSHI FLOWERS) (INDIAN)											
Jar	200										
INDIVIDUAL SALT DIP											
Salt Dip	75										

Pattern Name	M	A	G	B	PO	AO	IB	IG	W	Red	Other
INDUSTRIA ARGENTINA STAR											
Bowl	85										
Plate, small	125										
Plate, 15", chop size	300										
Vase	225										
INSULATOR (VARIOUS MAKERS)											
Various sizes	15+										
INTAGLIO DAISY (DIAMOND)											
Bowl, 4½"	30	90									
Bowl, 7½"	50	150									
INTAGLIO FEATHERS											
Cup	25										
INTAGLIO OVALS (U.S. GLASS)											
Bowl, 7"											75 PM
Plate, 7½"											100 PM
INTAGLIO STARS											
Tumbler, rare	600										
INTAGLIO THISTLE											
Bowl, scarce	125										
INTERIOR FLUTE											
Creamer	50										
Sugar	60										
INTERIOR PANELS											
Decanter	65										
Mug	75										
INTERIOR POINSETTIA (NORTHWOOD)											
Tumbler, rare	400										
INTERIOR RAYS (U.S. GLASS) (DEPRESSION ERA)											
Many shapes and sizes from $5 to $50											
INTERIOR RIB											
Vase	50										50 SM
INTERIOR SMOOTH PANEL (JEFFERSON)											
Spittoon, rare						1500					
INTERIOR SWIRL											
Tumbler	50		70								
Spittoon					140						
Vase, footed, 9"	40										
INTERIOR SWIRL AND WIDE PANEL											
Squat Pitcher	75										
INTERIOR WIDE PANELS (FENTON)											
Pitcher	175										
Tumbler	30										
INVERTED COIN DOT (FENTON)											
Pitcher, rare	100										
Tumbler, scarce	25										
INVERTED COIN DOT (NORTHWOOD)											
Tumbler, very rare	300										
INVERTED DIAMONDS											
Double Salt Dip	125										
INVERTED FEATHER (CAMBRIDGE)											
Bonbon Whimsey (from cracker jar), very rare			2700								
Compote	75										
Covered Butter, rare	450	500									
Cracker Jar w/lid		750	300								
Creamer, Sugar, or Spooner, rare	400	450									
Cup, rare	75										
Parfait	60										
Punch Bowl w/base, rare	3000		4600								
Pitcher, tall, rare	4500	6500									
Pitcher, squat, rare	1600										
Tumbler, rare	450	575	675								
Wine, rare	375										
INVERTED PRISMS (ENGLISH)											
Creamer	70										
Sugar, open	60										
INVERTED STRAWBERRY (CAMBRIDGE)											
Bonbon, stemmed w/handle, rare			900								
Bonbon Whimsey from spooner, two handled, rare			1700								
Bowl, 5"	40	115	75								
Bowl, 7"		235		125							
Bowl, 7½", square, rare				450							
Bowl, 9" – 10½"	145	235	275	375							
Candlesticks, pair, scarce	425	475	950								
Celery, very scarce		600	900	1000							
Compote, small, very scarce	400			900							
Compote, large, very scarce	225	325	450	1300							
Compote Whimsey, rare	1500										
Covered Butter	850	1100									
Creamer, Sugar, or Spooner, each, rare	375	225	325	425							

Pattern Name	M	A	G	B	PO	AO	IB	IG	W	Red	Other
Hat Whimsey, rare				950							
Ladies Spittoon, rare	900	1350	1800								
Milk Pitcher, rare		5000									
Powder Jar, very scarce	200		325								
Pitcher, rare	2200	2400	2000								
Rose Bowl, 8", rare	550	850									
Tumbler, rare	135	165	200	500							
Tumbler Whimsey, four sided, rare				1200							
Table Set, two pieces (stemmed), rare		1300									
INVERTED THISTLE (CAMBRIDGE)											
Bowl, 5", rare		150	150								
Bowl, 9", rare		325	325								
Bowl, Whimsey, footed, rare			600								
Butter, rare	500	600	700								
Chop Plate, rare		2700									
Compote, 8", rare			2000								
Covered Box, rare				400							
Creamer, Sugar, or Spooner, rare	350	400	500								
Milk Pitcher, rare		2700	2900								
Pitcher, rare	3000	1800									
Tumbler, rare	350	350									
Spittoon, rare		4000									
INWALD'S DIAMOND CUT											
Bowl (jardiniere)				400							
Vase	475										
INWALD'S PINWHEEL											
Vase, 5"	150										
INWALD STARS											
Pitcher	300										
IOWA											
Small Mug, rare	100										
IRIS (FENTON)											
Buttermilk Goblet	25	65	65	125							80 AM
Compote	50	60	60	90					235		
ISAAC BENESCH (MILLERSBURG)											
Bowl, advertising, 6½"		425									
Misspelled version, rare		1000									
ISIS											
Tumbler, rare	150										
ISLANDER ASHTRAY											
Ashtray, scarce	100										
IVY											
Stemmed Claret	85										
Stemmed Wine	75										
I.W. HARPER											
Decanter w/stopper	85										
JACK-IN-THE-PULPIT (DUGAN)											
Vase	45	75		80	125						
JACK-IN-THE-PULPIT (NORTHWOOD)											
Vase	50	175	200	275		375			100		
Vase, advertising, very rare						600			150		
JACKMAN											
Whiskey Bottle	50										
JACOBEAN (INWALD)											
Decanter	200										
Tumbler, three sizes	40 – 125										
Tray	95										
JACOBEAN RANGER (CZECH AND ENGLISH)											
Bowls, various shapes	60+										
Decanter w/stopper	200										
Juice Tumbler	125										
Miniature Tumbler	150										
Pitcher	325										
Tumbler	90										
Wine	40										
JACOB'S LADDER											
Perfume	60										
JACOB'S LADDER VARIANT (U.S. GLASS)											
Rose Bowl	85										
JAMIE'S JUG (AKA: DIAMOND TOP)											
Creamer	125										
JASMINE AND BUTTERFLY (CZECH)											
Decanter	100										
Guest Set, complete	200										
Tumbler	25										
JEANNETTE COLONIAL											
Rose Bowl, 5½"	30										
JEANNETTE REFRIGERATOR JAR											
Jar, covered	50										
JELLY JAR											
Complete	65										
JENKINS LATTICE (#336)											
Spooner	75										

Pattern Name	M	A	G	B	PO	AO	IB	IG	W	Red	Other
JESTER'S CAP (DUGAN/DIAMOND)											
Vase	45	75			100						200 CeB
JESTER'S CAP (NORTHWOOD)											
Vase	85	175	175	225							250 TL
JESTER'S CAP (WESTMORELAND)											
Vase	75	100	100		200	300 BO					150 TL
JEWEL BOX											
Ink Well	150		200								
JEWELED BUTTERFLIES (INDIANA)											
Bowl, square, rare	225										
JEWELED HEART (DUGAN)											
Basket Whimsey, rare					450						
Bowl, 5"		40			65				65		
Bowl, 10"		95			135				250		
Plate, 6"	150	175			200						
Pitcher, rare	900										
Tumbler, rare	100								575		
JEWELED PEACOCK TAIL											
Vase, 8", rare		375									
JEWELED SUNFLOWER											
Vase, scarce	155										
JEWEL'S (DUGAN)											
Bowl, various sizes		50	150	175						200	80 CeB
Candle Bowl	85							175			
Candlesticks, pair	100	150	175	200						275	150 CeB
Vase	75	150	150	175						200	200 AM
JEWEL'S AND DRAPERY (NORTHWOOD)											
Vase, rare			325								
JEWEL WITH DEWDROP											
Toothpick Holder	100										
JOCKEY CLUB (NORTHWOOD)											
Bowl, very scarce		1500									
Plate, flat or handgrip, scarce		1800									
JOSEF'S PLUMES											
Pitcher, rare	1250										
Vase, 6"	650										
J.R. MILNER CO., LYNCHBURG, VA											
See Cosmos and Cane (U.S. Glass)											
KALEIDOSCOPE											
Bowl, 8" – 9", scarce	65										
KANGAROO (AUSTRALIAN)											
Bowl, 5"	100	180									
Bowl, 9½"	300	500									
KAREN											
Bowl, small, rare	90										
Bowl, large, rare	275										
KARVE (FINLAND)											
Vase, 7"											200 LV
KATHLEEN'S FLOWERS (INDIA) (AKA: FANTASY FLOWERS)											
Tumbler	165										
KEDVESH (INDIA)											
Vase	200										
KEYHOLE (DUGAN)											
Bowl, 9½", very scarce	300	375			350						
*Also exterior of Raindrops bowl											
KEYSTONE COLONIAL (WESTMORELAND)											
Compote, 6¼", scarce	300	300									
KINGFISHER AND VARIANT (AUSTRALIAN)											
Bowl, 5"	95	185									
Bowl, 9½"	225	325									
Jardiniere, from large bowl, very rare		800									
KING'S CROWN (U.S. GLASS)											
Stemmed Wine	30										
KITTEN											
Miniature Paperweight, rare	250										
KITTENS											
Bottle											65 PM
KITTENS (FENTON)											
Bowl, two sides up, scarce	145	500		300							250 LV
Bowl, four sides up, scarce	145			300							350 AQ
Cereal Bowl, scarce	175	250		350							375 LV
Cup, scarce	125			400							
Plate, 4½", scarce	165	300		325							650 V
Ruffled Bowl, scarce	125			350							285 AQ
Saucer, scarce	165			325							250 PB
Spooner or Toothpick Holder	135			225							500 V
Spittoon Whimsey, very rare	4500			7000							
Vase, 3", scarce	105			235							
KIWI AND VARIANT (AUSTRALIAN)											
Bowl, 5", rare	250	200									
Bowl, 10", rare	350	1000									

53

Pattern Name	M	A	G	B	PO	AO	IB	IG	W	Red	Other
KNIGHTS TEMPLAR											
See Dandelion (Northwood)											
KNOTTED BEADS (FENTON)											
Vase, 4" – 12"	25	65	60	80						725	250 AM
KOKOMO (ENGLISH)											
Bowl, 8"	55										
Rose Bowl, footed	75										
KOOKABURRA (AUSTRALIAN)											
Bowl, 5"	175	225									165 BA
Bowl, 9"	425	1300									
Bowl, 9", lettered, very rare	1500										
KOOKABURRA FLOAT BOWL											
Bowl, 10" – 11", round or ruffled, rare	900	2300									
KRYS-TOL COLONIAL (JEFFERSON)											
Mayonnaise Set, two pieces	125										
KULOR (SWEDEN)											
Vase, 6" – 8", very scarce	1100	4000		2000							3000 TL
LA BELLE ROSE											
Bowl, 5", rare	200										
LACO											
Oil Bottle, 9¼"	80										
LACEY DAISY											
Vase, 10", very scarce	250										
LACY DEWDROP (WESTMORELAND)											
*All pieces, scarce, rare											
Banana Boat											350 IM
Bowl, covered											300 IM
Cake Plate											200 IM
Compote, covered											450 IM
Goblet											225 IM
Pitcher											650 IM
Tumbler											175 IM
Sugar											175 IM
(Note: all items listed are in Pearl Carnival)											
LADDERS (IMPERIAL)											
Bowl, 8", very scarce	100										
LADY'S SLIPPER											
One shape, rare	250										
LAKE SHORE HONEY											
Honey Jar, one size	200										
LANCASTER COMPOTE											
Compote									150		
LANGERKRANS (SWEDEN)											
Candy w/lid, 5"	125										
LARGE KANGAROO (AUSTRALIAN)											
Bowl, 5"	60	75									
Bowl, 10"	300	450									
LATE COVERED SWAN											
One Shape w/lid				550							
LATE ENAMELED BLEEDING HEARTS											
Tumbler	175										
LATE ENAMELED GRAPE											
Goblet	100										
LATE ENAMELED STRAWBERRY											
Lemonade Tumbler	75										
LATE FEATHER											
Pitcher	55										
Tumbler	15										
LATE STRAWBERRY											
Pitcher	225										
Tumbler	75										
LATE WATER LILY											
Pitcher	50										
Tumbler	20										
LATTICE (CRYSTAL)											
Bowl, 7" – 8"	100	145									
LATTICE (DUGAN)											
Bowls, various sizes	60	70									85 LV
LATTICE AND DAISY (DUGAN)											
Bowl, 5"	30								100		
Bowl, 9"	65										
Pitcher	175	1200		1600							
Tumbler	20	90		80					200		
LATTICE AND GRAPE (FENTON)											
Pitcher	225			450	2200				1600		
Tumbler	30			45	500				145		100 PB
Spittoon Whimsey, rare	3500										
LATTICE AND LEAVES											
Vase, 9½"	275			300							
LATTICE AND POINTS (DUGAN)											
Vase	40	95		225	175				100		
LATTICE AND PRISMS											
Cologne w/stopper	65										

Pattern Name	M	A	G	B	PO	AO	IB	IG	W	Red	Other
LATTICE AND SPRAYS											
Vase, 10½"	50										
LATTICE HEART											
Bowl, 6½" – 7½"		175									200 BA
Plate, 7" – 8"		300									325 BA
LAUREL											
Shade	40										
LAUREL AND GRAPE											
Vase, 6"					120						
LAUREL BAND											
Pitcher	95										
Tumbler	40										
LAUREL CLUSTER											
Tray	100										
LAUREL LEAVES (IMPERIAL)											
Compote	65										
Plate	40	55									65 SM
LAUREL WREATH											
Compote, 5"	65										
LBJ HAT											
Ashtray	25										
LEA (SOWERBY)											
Bowl, footed	40										
Creamer or Sugar, footed	45	50									
Pickle Dish, handled	45										
LEAF AND BEADS (NORTHWOOD)											
Bowl, dome footed	50	80	70								
Candy Dish, three footed	40	100	85	325		700					
Nut Bowl, footed, scarce	110	125	85	300		1750			325		1500 SM
Plate Whimsey, rare	150		200								
Rose Bowl, footed	135	150	165	225		350	1100	1450	500		1700 GO
Rose Bowl, sawtooth edge, very scarce	300	425		535							
Rose Bowl, smooth edge, very scarce	285	400									1400 IC
(Add 25% for patterned interior)											
LEAF AND CHRYSANTHEMUM											
Bowl	115										
LEAF AND LITTLE FLOWERS (MILLERSBURG)											
Compote, miniature, rare	325	500	525								
LEAF AND STAR (NEW MARTINSVILLE)											
Toothpick Holder	125										
Tumbler	95										
LEAF CHAIN (FENTON)											
Bowl, 7" – 9"	30	125	100	85		2500		2600	85	1100	225 LV
Plate, 7½"	70		325	150				4100			135 CM
Plate, 9¼"	360	2500	300	875					200		5100 Y
LEAF COLUMN (NORTHWOOD)											
Shade											100 AM
Vase	75	115	250	950			1400	450	325		255 HO
LEAF FAN											
Open Sugar	75										
LEAF GARDEN (IMPERIAL)											
Shade, very scarce	85										300 SM
LEAF RAYS (DUGAN)											
Nappy, spade shape	30	40		375	45			225	85		100 LV
Nappy, ruffled, scarce	65	125			90				90		125 LV
(Add 10% for Daisy May exterior)											
LEAF ROSETTES AND BEADS (DUGAN)											
*Same as Flowers and Beads											
Bowl, 6" – 7"	30	60			75						
Plate, 7", hex shape	75	110			125						
LEAF SWIRL (WESTMORELAND)											
Compote	50	70		80 TL							145 Y
Goblet shape	60	80		95 TL							160 Y
LEAF SWIRL AND FLOWER (FENTON)											
Vase	50								65		
LEAF TIERS (FENTON)											
Banana Bowl Whimsey	200										
Bowl, footed, 5"	30										
Bowl, footed, 10"	60			2000							
Butter, footed	175										
Creamer, Spooner, footed	75										
Plate Whimsey, from spooner	450										
Sugar, footed	90										
Pitcher, footed, rare	525			725							
Tumbler, footed, rare	125			165							
LEAFY TRIANGLE											
Bowl, 7"	55										
LEA VARIANT (SOWERBY)											
Creamer, footed	50										
LIBERTY BELL											
Bank	20										
Cookie Jar w/lid	40										

Pattern Name	M	A	G	B	PO	AO	IB	IG	W	Red	Other
LIGHTNING FLOWER (NORTHWOOD)											
Bowl, 5", rare	100										
Nappy, rare	125										
Nappy Variant (Proof — absentee design in flowers and leaves), very rare	350										
LIGHTOLIER LUSTRE AND CLEAR											
Shade	55										
LILY OF THE VALLEY (FENTON)											
Pitcher, rare				7000							
Tumbler, rare	525			225							
LILY VASE (AUSTRALIAN)											
Vase, 9" – 13"											800 BA
LINDAL											
Vase, 4" – 5", mini	200										
LINED LATTICE (DUGAN)											
Vase, squat, 5" – 7"	225	250		425	300				200		325 HO
Vase, 8" – 12"	80	200		350	250				125		275 HO
LINED LATTICE VARIANT (DUGAN)											
Vase, 9" – 16"	75	125			250						150 BA
LINCOLN DRAPE											
Mini Lamp, rare	1000										
LINN'S MUMS (NORTHWOOD)											
Bowl, footed, very rare		1800									
LION (FENTON)											
Bowl, 7", scarce	115			300							250 PB
Plate, 7½", rare	1300										
LITTLE BARREL (IMPERIAL)											
One Shape	150		200								200 SM
LITTLE BEADS											
Bowl, 8"	20				45						
Compote, small	30	40			65	85					70 AQ
LITTLE DAISIES (FENTON)											
Bowl, 8" – 9½", rare	1200			1400							
LITTLE DAISY											
Lamp, complete, 8"											500 AM
LITTLE DARLING											
Bottle	50										
LITTLE FISHES (FENTON)											
Bowl, flat or footed, 5½"	95	145		150					350		200 AQ
Bowl, flat or footed, 10"	175	425		425				8000	1500		
Plate, 10½", rare	5000										
LITTLE FLOWERS (FENTON)											
Bowl, 5½" "	25	40	85	65							75 AQ
Bowl, 6", ice cream shape	40	50	95	75							
Bowl, 5½", square, rare	150										
Bowl, 6", tricorner	125	175									
Bowl, 9½"	70	175	165	145							1000 AB
Bowl, 10", ice cream shape, very scarce		175		250						4300	250 PB
Plate, 7", rare	165										
Plate, 10", rare	2500										
LITTLE JEWEL											
Finger Lamp, rare	650										
LITTLE MERMAID											
One Shape											100 AM
LITTLE STARS (MILLERSBURG)											
Bowl, 6", ice cream shape, rare		700	825	2500							
Bowl, 7" – 7½", scarce	125	150	300	3000							125 CM
Bowl, 8" – 9", scarce	350	450	450								400 CM
Bowl, 10½", rare	600	700	800	4200							
Plate, 7½", rare	1150	1400	1600								
LITTLE SWAN											
Miniature, 3"											75 AM
LOGANBERRY (IMPERIAL)											
Whimsey Vase, scarce		2500									
Vase, scarce	325	2200	550								775 AM
LOG CABIN SYRUP											
Cabin Shaped Syrup, rare	325										
LOG PAPERWEIGHT											
Novelty, 3" x 1¼", rare	150										
LONG BUTTRESS											
Pitcher	400										
Tumbler	250										
Toothpick	200										
LONG HOBSTAR (IMPERIAL)											
Bowl, 8½"	45										
Bowl, 10½"	60										
Compote	65										
Punch Bowl w/base	125										150 CM
LONG HORN											
Wine	60										
LONG LEAF (DUGAN)											
Bowl, footed					175						
LONG THUMBPRINT (FENTON)											
Vase, 7" – 11"	30	35	45	100							
Vase Whimsey	75										

Pattern Name	M	A	G	B	PO	AO	IB	IG	W	Red	Other
LONG THUMBPRINT HOBNAIL (FENTON)											
Vase, 7" – 11"	50	65	75	130							
LONG THUMBPRINT VARIANT											
Bowl, 8¾"	30	40									
Butter	75										
Compote	30	40	40								
Creamer or Sugar, each	40										50 SM
LOTUS (FENTON)											
Pitcher	400										
Tumbler	35										
LOTUS AND GRAPE (FENTON)											
Absentee Bowl, rare				1900							
Bonbon	40	110	150	85						1200	225 V
Bowl, flat, 7" – 8½"	65	70	165	125							375 PeB
Plate, 9½", rare	7000	2200	1800	1400							
LOTUS AND GRAPE VARIANT (FENTON)											
Bonbon, footed, scarce	45	110	150	100						600	
Bowl, footed, 6"	40	75	90	80							
Rose Bowl, footed, scarce	425			500							
LOTUS BUD (INDIA)											
Vase	195										
LOTUS LAND (NORTHWOOD)											
Bonbon, rare	1500	750									
LOUISA (WESTMORELAND)											
Bowl, footed		95	75		135						65 AQ
Candy Dish, footed	50	85	65								70 AQ
Mini Banana Boat (old only)	45	70									
Nut Bowl, scarce		250									
Plate, footed, 8", rare	100	165			350						125 AQ
Rose Bowl	50	70	65	175							75 TL
LOUISA (JEANNETTE)											
*Floragold Depression name, many shapes and sizes, prices from $10 to $650, late 1950s											
LOVEBIRDS											
Bottle w/stopper	575										
LOVE BIRDS (CONSOLIDATED)											
Vase, very rare								450		600	375 SM
LOVELY (NORTHWOOD)											
Bowl, footed		900	1100								
LOVING CUP (FENTON)											
Loving Cup, scarce	225	700	400	325	7000	15000			550		
*Part of the Orange Tree line											
LUCILE											
Pitcher, rare	1200			1000							
Tumbler, rare	450			250							
LUCKY BANK											
One shape	35										
LUCKY BELL											
Bowl, 4", rare	65										
Bowl, 8¾", rare	135										
LULES ARGENTINA											
Plate	225										
LUSTRE											
Tumbler	45										
LUSTRE AND CLEAR (FENTON)											
Fan Vase	40		60	55				90			
LUSTRE AND CLEAR (IMPERIAL)											
Bowl, 5"	20										
Bowl, 10"	25										
Butter Dish	65										
Console Set, three pieces	60									375	
Creamer or Sugar	25	65	150								30 CM
Pitcher	145										
Tumbler	40										
Rose Bowl	75										
Shakers, pair	75										
LUSTRE FLUTE (NORTHWOOD)											
Bonbon		50	50								
Bowl, 5½"	25	30	30								
Bowl, 8"	50	65	65								
Compote		55	50								
Creamer or Sugar	40	55	55								
Hat	25	30	30								
Nappy (from punch cup)	50	75	70								
Punch Cup	20	25	20								
Sherbet	35										
LUSTRE MATCH SAFE (FENTON)											
Match Safe	70										
LUSTRE ROSE (IMPERIAL)											
Bowl, Fruit, footed, 11" – 12"	40	750	125							2000	1500 V
Bowl, Berry, footed, 5"	20	55	30	125							20 CM
Bowl, Berry, footed, 8" – 10"	35	225	50								40 CM
Bowl, centerpiece, footed	100	425	200								250 SM

Pattern Name	M	A	G	B	PO	AO	IB	IG	W	Red	Other
Butter	70	250	70								225 AM
Creamer, Sugar, or Spooner	35	150	40								100 PB
Fernery	40	200	120	75							125 PB
Milk Pitcher	100										125 CM
Plate Whimsey, footed	250										200 CM
Pitcher	125	600	225								350 AM
Tumbler	20	100	40								140 CM
Tumbler Whimsey, rare											525 AM
LUTTICH											
Vase	125										
LUTZ (MCKEE)											
Mug, footed	100										
MADAY AND CO.											
See Wild Blackberry											
MADHU (INDIA)											
Tumbler	150										
MADONNA (INDIA)											
Pitcher	350										
Tumbler	95										
MAE'S DAISIES (GRAPEVINE AND FLOWER) (INDIA)											
Tumbler	150										
MAE WEST (DUGAN)											
Candlesticks, each											150 CeB
MAGNOLIA DRAPE (FENTON)											
Pitcher	200										
Tumbler	35										
MAGNOLIA RIB (FENTON)											
Berry Bowl, small	20										
Berry Bowl, large	55										
Butter	125										
Creamer or Spooner	60										
Sugar w/lid	75										
MAGPIE AND VARIANT (AUSTRALIAN)											
Bowl, 5"	95	200									
Bowl, 8" – 10"	250	475									
MAHARAJAH (JAIN)											
Shot Glass, rare	175										
MAIZE (LIBBEY)											
Syrup (cruet), rare											235 CL
Vase, celery, rare											185 CL
MAJESTIC (MCKEE)											
Tumbler, rare	500										
MALAGA (DIAMOND)											
Bowl, 9", scarce	75	150									
Plate, 10", rare		500									400 AM
Rose Bowl, rare	125	400									
MALLARD DUCK											
One shape											550 CRAN
MANCHESTER											
Flower Holder w/frog											100 AM
MANHATTAN (U.S. GLASS)											
Decanter	300										
Plate, 6"	65										
Tray	125										
Wine	45										
Vase, rare	325										
MANY DIAMONDS											
Ice Bucket	225										
Tumbler	60										
MANY FLUTES											
Compote	100										
MANY FRUITS (DUGAN)											
Punch Bowl w/base	400	700		2500					1400		
Punch Cup	25	30	40	125					70		
MANY PRISMS											
Perfume w/stopper	75										
MANY RIBS (MODEL FLINT-NORTHWOOD)											
Vase, 8", very rare						3000					
MANY STARS AND VARIANT (MILLERSBURG)											
Bowl, ruffled, 9", scarce	375	500	550	3000							3000 V
Bowl, ice cream shape, 9½", rare	475	1100	1100	4250							
Bowl, tricornered, rare		2500									
Chop Plate, very rare	5000										
MAPLE LEAF (DUGAN)											
Bowl, stemmed, 4½"	30	35	50	40							
Bowl, stemmed, 9"	60	100		100							
Butter	125	150		150							
Creamer or Spooner	45	55		70							
Sugar	70	80		90							
Pitcher	175	300		350							
Tumbler	25	40		55							300 PB
MAPLE LEAF BASKET											
Basket, handled, large	65										

Pattern Name	M	A	G	B	PO	AO	IB	IG	W	Red	Other
MARDI GRAS											
Butter Dish, small	150										
MARGUERITE											
Vase, 10"	110										
MARIANNA (CZECH)											
Vase	260										
MARIE (FENTON)											
Rustic vase interior base pattern											
MARILYN (MILLERSBURG)											
Pitcher, rare	950	1350	2000								
Tumbler, rare	135	225	350								
MARTEC (MCKEE)											
Tumbler, rare	500										
MARTHA											
Compote, 7½"	160										
MARY ANN (DUGAN)											
Vase, two varieties, 7"	100	375									
Loving Cup, three handled, rare	550										1000 PkA
MARY GREGORY											
Cologne Bottle, rare	175										
MASSACHUSETTS (U.S. GLASS)											
Mug, rare	150										
Tumbler, very scarce	200										
Vase, very scarce	175										
MAYAN (MILLERSBURG)											
Bowl, 8½" – 10"	3500		150								
*(Common in green, all others, rare)											
MAY BASKET											
Basket, 7½"	40		95								
Bowl, 9", rare			160								
MAYFLOWER (IMPERIAL)											
Light Shade	45		70								100 SM
MAYFLOWER (MILLERSBURG)											
Bowl, 9" – 9½", very rare	3000										
Exterior of Grape Leaves bowls											
MAYPOLE											
Vase, 6¼"	45	105	60								
MCKEE'S #20											
Sherbet	35										
MCKEE'S SQUIGGY											
Vase	90		125								
MEANDER (NORTHWOOD)											
Exterior only											
MELON RIB											
Candy Jar w/lid	30										
Decanter	90										
Powder Jar w/lid	35										
Pitcher	60										
Tumbler	20										
Shakers, pair	35										
MELON RIB GENIE											
Vase, 5"		150									
MELTING ICE											
Vase, 8½", scarce	200										
MEMPHIS (NORTHWOOD)											
Berry Bowl, 5"	35	45									
Berry Bowl, 10" – 12"	125	350				5100					
Fruit Bowl w/base	325	400	800	2400			4000	6000	1200		2600 LG
Hat Whimsey, from tumbler, very rare	900										
Punch Bowl w/base	450	625	2300				4500	15000	2100		65 LG
Punch Cup	25	40	50				85	95			
Shakers, each, rare			200								
METALICA											
Covered Candy w/metal filagree work	50										
METRO											
Vase, 9" – 14", rare	275										
MEXICALI VASE											
Vase, footed, 8"	90										
MEXICAN BELL											
Goblet, flashed	40										
MEYDAM (LEERDAM)											
Butter	135										
Cake Stand	95										
Compote	75										
MIKADO (FENTON)											
Compote, large	200	850	1750	600					1000	9000	600 PB
MIKE'S MYSTERY											
Bowl, 8½"	135										
MILADY (FENTON)											
Pitcher	650	2500	2900	1200							
Tumbler	85	100	325	125							
MILLER FURNITURE (FENTON)											
Open Edge Basket, advertising	50		125								
MILLERSBURG FOUR PILLARS											
Vase, star base, rare	300	250	350								

Pattern Name	M	A	G	B	PO	AO	IB	IG	W	Red	Other
MILLERSBURG FOUR PILLARS VARIANT											
Vase, swirled, plain base, rare		500									
MILLERSBURG GRAPE											
Bowl, 5"	40										
Bowl, 8½"	90		900								
MINIATURE BATHTUB											
One Shape	150										
MINIATURE BEAKER											
Souvenir Mini Beaker, rare	100										
MINIATURE BEAN POT (CZECH)											
One shape, 2½"	80										
MINIATURE BEER MUG											
Mug, miniature	75										
MINIATURE BELL											
Paperweight, 2½"	60										
MINIATURE BLACKBERRY (FENTON)											
Compote, small	80	125	200	75					525		
Compote, absentee variant	60	85	95	90							
Stemmed Plate, very scarce				450					450		
MINIATURE BOTTLE											
Bottle	40										
MINIATURE CANDELABRA (CAMBRIDGE)											
One size	500										
MINIATURE CHILD'S SHOE											
One shape	325										
MINIATURE COMPOTE											
Compote, 2½"								90			
MINIATURE COW											
One size	700										
MINIATURE FLOWER BASKET (WESTMORELAND)											
Basket				150							300 BO
MINIATURE HOBNAIL											
Pitcher, 6", rare	250										
Tumbler, 2½"	50										
MINIATURE HOBNAIL (EUROPEAN)											
Cordial Set, rare	1250										
Nut Cup, stemmed, rare	400								550		
(Also known as Wild Rose Wreath)											
MINIATURE LACED BOOT											
Miniature Boot	125										
MINIATURE LOVING CUP											
One Size	75										
MINIATURE NAPPY											
Two Handled Nappy	75										
MINIATURE PANELED MUG											
Mug, miniature	75										
MINIATURE ROSE BOWL											
One Shape, 4"	30										
MINIATURE SANDAL											
One Shape	500										
MINIATURE SHELL											
Candleholder, each											75 CL
MINIATURE SHERBET											
Stemmed Sherbet, 3"	60										
MINIATURE SWIRL											
Mini Bottle, 2¾" tall	50										
MINIATURE URN											
One Shape	40										
MINIATURE WASH BOWL AND PITCHER											
Bowl, 3⅝"	55										
Pitcher, 2¾"	70										
MINI DIAMOND AND FILE BAND											
Shakers, each	45										
MINI DIAMONDS (INDIA)											
Juice Tumbler	125										
MINI SAWTOOTH SHAKER											
Miniature Shaker, each	50										
MINNESOTA (U.S. GLASS)											
Mug	100										
Toothpick Holder	60										
MINUET (LATE)											
Pitcher	75										
Tumbler	20										
MIRROR AND CROSSBAR (JAIN)											
Tumbler, rare	290										
MIRRORED LOTUS (FENTON)											
Bowl, 7" – 8½"	75			165				2500			3000 CeB
Plate, 7½", rare	500			650							4900 CeB
Rose Bowl, rare	325			500					600		
MIRRORED PEACOCKS (JAIN)											
Tumbler, rare	325										

Pattern Name	M	A	G	B	PO	AO	IB	IG	W	Red	Other
MIRRORED VEES (RINDSKOPF)											
Tumbler, very scarce	175										
MISTY MORN (JAIN)											
Vase	675										
MITERED BLOCK (EUROPEAN)											
Lamp, scarce	195										
MITERED DIAMOND AND PLEATS (ENGLISH)											
Bowl, 4½"	25			30							
Bowl, shallow, 8½"	40			45							
Rose Bowl Whimsey	95										
MITERED MAZE											
Vase, 12"										300	200 SM
MITERED OVALS (MILLERSBURG)											
Vase, rare	9000	10000	8000								
MODERNE											
Cup or Saucer	15										
MOLLER (EDA)											
Bowl	210			325							
Rose Bowl	350			500							
MONKEY BOTTLE											
Bottle, 4¾"	250										
MONSOON (INDIA)											
Pitcher	285										
Tumbler	80										
MOON AND STAR (WESTMORELAND)											
Compote (Pearl carnival)											385 IC
MOON AND STARS BAND											
Pitcher	450										
Tumbler	100										
MOONGLEAM (HEISEY)											
Pitcher w/lid, rare			400								
Tumbler, rare			30								
MOONPRINT (BROCKWITZ)											
Banana Boat, rare	135										
Bowl, 8½"	45										
Bowl, 14"	80										
Butter	100										
Candlesticks, each, rare	90										
Cheese Keeper, rare	175										
Compote	55										
Cordial	35										
Creamer	40										
Decanter w/stopper	250										
Jar w/lid	65										
Pitcher, squat, scarce	225										
Sugar, stemmed	50										
Tray	75										
Vase, very scarce	400										
MORNING GLORY (IMPERIAL)											
Vase, squat, 4" – 7"	65	135	120								125 SM
Vase, standard, 8" – 15"	55	225	125								145 SM
Vase, funeral, 13" – 22"	575	900	450	10000							250 SM
MORNING GLORY (MILLERSBURG)											
Pitcher, rare	18000	19000	21000								
Tumbler, rare	1000	2500	4000								
MOUNTAIN LAKE											
Lamp Shade	85										
MOXIE											
Bottle, rare										90	
MT. GAMBIER (CRYSTAL)											
Mug	100										
Mug, Quorum	125										
MULTI-FRUITS AND FLOWERS (MILLERSBURG)											
Dessert, stemmed, rare		900	900								
Punch Bowl w/base, flared, rare	1800	2100	3900	25000							
Punch Bowl w/base, Tulip top, rare	3800	4300	4900	55000							
Punch Cup, rare	60	85	100	900							
Pitcher (either base), rare	11000	8000	9000								
Tumbler, rare	900	1000	1200								
MUSCADINE (JAIN)											
Tumbler, rare	275										
MUSCADINE VARIANT (JAIN)											
Tumbler	300										
MY LADY											
Powder Jar w/lid	125										
MYSTERY											
Perfume	50										
MYSTERY GRAPE											
Bowl			175								
MYSTIC (CAMBRIDGE)											
Vase, footed, rare	175										
MYSTIC GRAPE											
Decanter w/stopper, 10½", rare	475										

Pattern Name	M	A	G	B	PO	AO	IB	IG	W	Red	Other
NANNA (EDA)											
Jardiniere	325			500							
Vase	350			575							
NAPCO #2255 (JEANNETTE)											
Compote	75										
NAPOLEON											
Bottle											85 CL
NAPOLI (ITALY)											
Decanter	75										
Wine	20			25			25				25 V
NARCISSUS AND RIBBON (FENTON)											
Wine Bottle w/stopper, rare	1200										
NAUTILUS (DUGAN-NORTHWOOD)											
Creamer or Sugar, scarce (lettered add 25%)		190			200						
Giant Compote, rare	3000										
Vase Whimsey, rare	300	400									
NAVAJO											
Vase, 7", very scarce	165										
NEAR-CUT (CAMBRIDGE)											
Decanter w/stopper, rare	2100		3000								
NEAR-CUT (NORTHWOOD)											
Compote	100	150	200								
Goblet, rare	175	125									
Pitcher, rare	3500										
Tumbler, rare	300	1200									
NEAR-CUT SOUVENIR (CAMBRIDGE)											
Mug, rare	200										
Tumbler, rare	275										
NEAR-CUT WREATH (MILLERSBURG)											
Exterior only											
NELL (HIGBEE)											
Mug	75										
NESTING SWAN (MILLERSBURG)											
Bowl, round or ruffled, 10", scarce	250	375	375	3100							700 HA
Bowl, square, rare			1500								
Bowl, tricornered, rare	550	1150	1300	3700							750 CM
Plate, 10", very rare			3500								
Proof Bowl, rare		2500	3200								
Rose Bowl, rare	4000										
Spittoon Whimsey, very rare		5000	5000								
NEW JERSEY (U.S. GLASS)											
Wine											100 HA
NEW ORLEANS SHRINE (U.S. GLASS)											
Champagne											150 CL
NEWPORT SHIP BOTTLE											
Bottle, one size			135								
NIAGARA FALLS (JEANNETTE)											
Milk Pitcher	35										
Pitcher	50										
Tumbler, three sizes	15										
NIGHTSHADE (CZECH)											
Bowl, dome based											165 CeB
NIGHT STARS (MILLERSBURG)											
Bonbon, rare	700	850	1400								1700 OG
Card Tray, rare	800	900	1200								
Nappy, tricornered, very rare	1500	1200	1800								
NIPPON (NORTHWOOD)											
Bowl, 8½"	150	450	600	500		21000	400	700	375		2000 HO
Plate, 9", scarce	800	925	1200				9000		1100		
NOLA (SCANDINAVIAN)											
Pitcher, squat	300										
Tumbler, two shapes	100										
Atomizer	125										
Perfume	80										
Basket, handled	65										
Tumble-up	250										
Ring Tray	50										
Powder Box w/lid, two sizes	75										
NORRIS N. SMITH (FENTON)											
Bowl, advertising, scarce		900									
Plate, advertising, 5¾", scarce		1800									
NORTHERN LIGHTS (BROCKWITZ)											
Bowl, two sizes	100 – 150			175 – 225							
Rose Bowl, two sizes	225 – 275			300 – 400							
NORTHERN STAR (FENTON)											
Bowl, 6"	30										
Bowl, 5", ice cream shape, scarce	75										
Bowl, tricorner	40										
Card Tray, 6"	40										
Plate, 6½", rare	100										

Pattern Name	M	A	G	B	PO	AO	IB	IG	W	Red	Other
NORTH STAR (LANCASTER)											
Punch Bowl, 15", top only	300										
*(No base has been found to date)											
NORTHWOOD #38 SHADE											
Lamp Shade									125		
NORTHWOOD #569											
Vase, various shapes	40	55		65							75 V
NORTHWOOD #637											
Compote (either shape)											125 CeB
NORTHWOOD #657											
Candlesticks, two sizes			100	135							150 V
NORTHWOOD #699											
Cheese Dish											100 V
Underplate											75 V
NORTHWOOD WIDE FLUTE											
Vase, midsize funeral, 8" – 15"	125	400	200	1000							150 ALS
NORTHWOOD WIDE PANEL											
Vase	80										335 V
NOTCHES											
Plate, 8"	50										
NU-ART CHRYSANTHEMUM (IMPERIAL)											
Plate, rare	900	3100	9250	12000					1700		25000 EG
(*Signed pieces, add 50%)											
NU-ART DRAPE (IMPERIAL)											
Shade	60										
NU-ART HOMESTEAD (IMPERIAL)											
Plate, scarce	650	2000	7000	10000							1400 LV
(*Signed pieces, add 50%)											
NU-ART PANELED SHADE (IMPERIAL)											
Shade, plain	50										
Shade, engraved	75										
NUGGET BEADS											
Beads		125									
NUMBER 110											
Mugs, various lettering	100										
NUMBER 195 (CROWN CRYSTAL)											
Sherbet	65										
NUMBER 221 (CROWN CRYSTAL)											
Bowl, 5"	65										
Bowl, 8½"	100										
NUMBER 270 (WESTMORELAND)											
Compote	50	90	140 RG		100 MMG	150 BO					110 AQ
Plate, from compote, very rare											200 AM
NUMBER 321 (CROWN CRYSTAL)											
Oval Bowl	125										
NUMBER 600 (FOSTORIA)											
Toothpick Holder	50										
NUMBER 2176 (SOWERBY)											
Lemon Squeezer	60										
NUTMEG GRATER											
Butter	125										
Creamer	55										
Sugar, open	55										
OAK LEAF LUSTRE (ARGENTINA)											
Butter	215										
Cheese Dish w/cover	140										
OCTAGON (IMPERIAL)											
Bowl, 4½"	20	40	35								
Bowl, 8½"	50	150	70								
Bowl, Fruit, 10" – 12"	75	250	150								
Butter	200	500	375								325 PB
Compote, two sizes	85	325									
Cordial	250										325 AQ
Creamer or Spooner	50	175	100								
Decanter, complete	110	500	750								
Goblet	50										100 AM
Handled Nappy, very scarce	200										
Milk Pitcher, scarce	100	350	250								150 CM
Pitcher, two sizes	225	650	400								500 SM
Tumbler	30										75 SM
Tumbler Variant	40	100	80								325 AQ
Rose Bowl, very rare	400										
Shakers, pair (old only)	325	525									
Sugar	60	225	100								
Toothpick Holder, rare	125	475									
Wine	65	100	150								200 PB
Vase, rare	100	200	150								75 CM
OCTET (NORTHWOOD)											
Bowl, 8½", scarce	100	135	170					325			
OGDEN FURNITURE (FENTON)											
Bowl, scarce		1350									
Plate, scarce		1000									
Plate, handgrip, scarce		1100									

Pattern Name	M	A	G	B	PO	AO	IB	IG	W	Red	Other
O'HARA (LOOP)											
Goblet	25										
Pitcher	120										
OHIO STAR (MILLERSBURG)											
Compote, tall, rare	1300										
Cloverleaf Shape Dish, very rare	3000										
Vase, very scarce	3000	2500	2800			25000			5000		
Vase Whimsey (stretched), very rare	10000	12000	14000								
OKLAHOMA (MEXICAN)											
Decanter	850										
Tumbler, rare	500										
OLD DOMINION											
Compote, 5⅜", scarce	40										
OLD FASHION											
Tray w/six tumblers, complete	150										
OLD GERMAN PIPE FLASK											
Novelty Flask, very rare									500		
OLD OAKEN BUCKET											
Novelty w/lid, complete	200										
OLYMPIC (MILLERSBURG)											
Compote, small, very rare		4800	5300								
OLYMPUS (NORTHWOOD)											
Bowl, very rare				12000							
Shade	125										
OMERA (IMPERIAL)											
Bowl, 6"	25										25 CM
Bowl, 8"	35										30 CM
Bowl, 10"	45								75		40 CM
Celery, handled	40										35 CM
Nappy, two handled	35										125 MMG
Plate, 8"	50									160	200 AM
Rose Bowl	75										60 CM
(Iron Cross add 25%)											
OMNIBUS											
Pitcher, very rare	700										
Tumbler, rare	200		400	550							
Pitcher Whimsey (no spout)			1200								
ONEATA *AKA: CHIMO (RIVERSIDE)											
Bowl, 9", rare	150										
OPEN EDGE BASKET											
BASKETWEAVE (FENTON)											
Bowl, small, either shape	30	150	150	50					160	325	150 SM
Bowl, large, either shape	75	175	175	70		300		375	190		450 CeB
Bowl, square, scarce	50	160	250	80						600	115 AQ
Bowl, tricorner, very scarce				200							
Hat, J.I.P. shape	25	125	180	40					125	375	225 AQ
Plate, rare	900			1400				1900	625		
Vase Whimsey, rare	800		1200							3000	
OPEN FLOWER (DUGAN)											
Bowl, flat or footed, 7"	35	45	50		85						
OPEN ROSE (IMPERIAL)											
Bowl, flat, 5½"	15	50	25	80							60 AQ
Bowl, flat, 9"	40	125	60	300							225 SM
Bowl, fruit, 10" – 12"	50	425	150							2200	200 SM
Plate, 9"	100	1800	525								225 AM
Rose Bowl	65	500	125								155 AM
OPTIC (IMPERIAL)											
Bowl, 6"	25	50									30 SM
Bowl, 9"	35	75									40 SM
Rose Bowl	80										100 SM
OPTIC AND BUTTONS (IMPERIAL)											
Bowls, 5" – 8"	30										40 CM
Bowl, handled, 12"	45										50 CM
Cup and Saucer, rare	300										250 CM
Goblet	60										90 LV
Plate, 10½"	70										75 CM
Pitcher, small, rare	185										200 CM
Tumbler, two shapes	50										40 CM
Rose Bowl	90										75 CM
Salt Cup, rare	200										
OPTIC BLOCK											
Plate	60										
OPTIC FLUTE (IMPERIAL)											
Bowl, 5"	20										35 SM
Bowl, 10"	35										50 SM
Compote	50										60 CM
Plate, 8", rare											200 CM
Spittoon Whimsey, scarce	225										
OPTIC RIB PITCHER											
Water Pitcher											65 AM
OPTIC VARIANT											
Bowl, 6"		90									
OPTIC 66 (FOSTORIA)											
Goblet	50										
ORANGE PEEL (WESTMORELAND)											
Custard Cup, scarce	25										

Pattern Name	M	A	G	B	PO	AO	IB	IG	W	Red	Other
Dessert, stemmed, scarce	45	70	80 RG								70 TL
Punch Bowl w/base	200	250									250 TL
Punch Cup	10	40									35 TL
ORANGE TREE (FENTON)											
Bowl, footed, 5½"	40		50	45					100		
Bowl, footed, 9" – 11"	100		175	125					200		
Bowl, flat, 8" – 9"	40	250	300	100			7400			2600	4000 CeB
Breakfast Set, two pieces	150	125	230	200					250		1500 IM
Butter	325			300					365		
Centerpiece Bowl, footed, 12", rare (from orange bowl)	900	4000	4500	1500							
Compote, regular size, banded	25		75	85							
Compote, small, without band			195								250 AM
Creamer or Spooner	45			65					125		
Creamer Whimsey from cup									195		
Cruet or Syrup Whimsey from mug, very rare				5000							
Hatpin Holder	350	750	2000	325					700		2700 ICG
Hatpin Holder Whimsey, rare				2600							
Ice Cream/Sherbet, short stemmed	25			35							
Loving Cup, scarce	225	700	400	325	7000	15000			550		
Mug, two sizes	35	150	475	65						475	275 TL
Orange Bowl (fruit bowl), footed, large	100	1600	4000	225							
Punch Bowl w/base	200		650	325	1000 MO				550		
Punch Cup	20		50	35					50		
Powder Jar w/lid	95	250	500	135					200		450 PB
Plate, 8" – 9½"	325	3000	4000	1100		17000			275		200 CM
Pitcher, two designs	300			850							18000 LO
Tumbler	40			75					110		
Rose Bowl (see Fenton's Flowers)											
Spittoon Whimsey, very rare	5500										
Sugar	60			70					125		
Wine, two sizes	25		275	30					60 AQ		125 V
Vase Whimsey, very rare				2300							
(Add 10% to bowls and plates for stylized flower center design)											
ORANGE TREE AND SCROLL (FENTON)											
Pitcher	475			900							
Tumbler	50			75							
ORANGE TREE ORCHARD (FENTON)											
Pitcher	400			600					425		
Tumbler	35			85					125		
Whimsey, handled, from pitcher, rare	7000										
ORBIT (INDIA)											
Vase, 9"	180			325							
ORCHID											
Pitcher									400		
Tumbler									65		
ORCHID VARIANT											
Pitcher	275										
Tumbler	40										
OREBRO (SWEDEN)											
Epergne, metal base	350										
Bowl, oval	80			185							
Bowl, round	65			125							
OREGON											
See Beaded Loop											
ORIENTAL POPPY (NORTHWOOD)											
Pitcher	400	900	1400	4500			3600	4300	1000		16000 SA
Pitcher, ribbed interior, rare	525										
Tumbler	40	90	95	200			175	250	165		
OSTRICH (CRYSTAL)											
Cake Stand, rare	325	450									
Compote, large, rare	265	385									
OVAL AND ROUND (IMPERIAL)											
Bowl, small	15	60	40								45 AM
Bowl, large	30	90	65								70 AM
Plate, 10", scarce	75	75	85								400 AM
Rose Bowl	125										
OWL BANK											
One Size	50										
OWL BOTTLE											
One Shape											65 CL
OXFORD											
Mustard Pot w/lid	75										
PACIFICA (U.S. GLASS)											
Tumbler	400										
PACIFIC COAST MAIL ORDER HOUSE											
See Grape and Cable (Fenton)											
PADEN CITY'S #198											
Syrup w/liner, rare	350										
PAGODA VASE											
Funeral Vase, 17", rare		800									
PAINTED CASTLE											
Shade	65										

Pattern Name	M	A	G	B	PO	AO	IB	IG	W	Red	Other
PAINTED PANSY											
Fan Vase	50										
PAINTED PEARL											
Bowl											275 IM
PALACE GATES (JAIN)											
Tumbler	300										
PALM BEACH (U.S. GLASS)											
Banana Bowl	100	175									175 HA
Bowl, 5" – 6"	100								95		90 HA
Bowl, 9"	55								120		40 HA
Butter	135								275		150 HA
Creamer or Spooner	75								125		75 HA
Plate, 9", rare	225	275							250		
Pitcher, scarce	325								600		500 HA
Tumbler, scarce	150								140		100 HA
Rose Bowl Whimsey, rare	350										150 LG
Sugar, covered	95										125 LG
Vase Whimsey, rare	785	500							900		
PALM LEAF											
Plate, handgrip, 6"	225										
PANAMA (U.S. GLASS)											
Goblet, rare	150										
Rose Bowl	575										
Spittoon	750										
PANDORA											
Bowl, 5½"	60										
PANELED (AUSTRALIAN)											
Sugar, open	80	100									
PANELED CANE											
Vase, 8"	250										
PANELED CRUET											
One Size	95										
PANELED DAISY AND CANE											
Basket, rare	700										
PANELED DANDELION (FENTON)											
Candle Lamp Whimsey, rare			3200								
Pitcher	285	400	575	525							
Tumbler	30	50	70	55							
Vase Whimsey from pitcher, rare				12500							
PANELED DIAMOND AND BOWS (FENTON)											
Vase, 5" – 12"	75	125	160	95						700	175 V
PANELED DIAMOND POINT AND FAN											
Bowl, rare	1350										
PANELED ELLIPSE											
Spittoon, 7½"	150										
PANELED FISH PALMS (INDIA)											
Vase, 5½"	150										
PANELED HOLLY (NORTHWOOD)											
Bonbon, footed	60	90	75								
Bowl		75	70								
Creamer or Sugar	65										
Pitcher, very rare		22000									
Spooner	55										
PANELED PALM (U.S. GLASS)											
Mug, rare	100										
Wine, rare	150										
PANELED PERFUME											
Perfume with Stopper	150										
PANELED PRISM											
Jam Jar w/lid	55										
PANELED ROSE (IMPERIAL)											
*Exterior only of Open Rose											
PANELED SMOCKING											
Creamer	55										
Sugar	50										
PANELED SWIRL											
Rose Bowl	65										
PANELED THISTLE (HIGBEE)											
Compote, rare	200										
Tumbler, very scarce	100										
PANELED TREE TRUNK (DUGAN)											
Vase, 7" – 12", rare		5250									
PANELED TWIGS											
Tumbler	200										
PANELS AND BALL (FENTON)											
(Also called Persian Pearl)											
Bowl, 11", scarce	60								175		
PANELS AND BEADS											
Shade											55 VO
PANELS AND DRAPERY (RIIHIMAKI)											
Bowl	70										
PANJI PEACOCK EYE (INDIA)											
Vase, 8½"	225										
PANSY (IMPERIAL)											
Bowl, 8¼"	45	165	95	350							240 SM

Pattern Name	M	A	G	B	PO	AO	IB	IG	W	Red	Other
Creamer or Sugar	25	60	50								125 SM
Dresser Tray	50	175	65								100 AM
Nappy (old only)	20	75	30	1300							85 LV
Pickle Dish, oval	30	80	40	275			425				70 SM
Plate, ruffled, scarce	100	325	200								125 SM
PANTHER (FENTON)											
Bowl, footed, 5"	25	225	350	115						850	350 AQ
Bowl, footed, 10"	225	500	485	400							800 AQ
Whimsey, footed, 5", scarce	200		500	375							200 CM
Whimsey, footed, 10", scarce	400			700							
(Note: whimsey pieces rest on collar base, feet are not touching)											
PAPERCHAIN											
Candlesticks, pair	80										
PAPERWEIGHT											
Flower-shaped, rare											200 PM
PAPINI VICTORIA (ARGENTINA)											
Compote	250										
Pitcher	375										
Tumbler	75										
PARADISE SODA (FENTON)											
Plate, advertising, scarce		500									
PARK AVENUE (FEDERAL)											
Pitcher, very scarce	100										
Tumbler, five sizes	5 – 20										
PARKERSBURG ELKS BELL (FENTON)											
1914 Parkersburg Bell, rare				2500							
PARLOR											
Ashtray				95							
PARLOR PANELS (IMPERIAL)											
Vase, 4" – 14"	110	325	110	900							475 AM
Vase Whimsey, swung top, rare											650 AM
PARQUET											
Creamer	70										
Sugar	80										
PASSION FLOWER											
Vase	125										
PASTEL HAT											
Various shapes and sizes	25+										25+ PB
PASTEL SWAN (DUGAN, FENTON, AND NORTHWOOD)											
One Size, regular shape	185	225	200	200	325		125	65	375		195 TL
Whimsey (head down touching neck), rare											1200 TL
PATRICIA (EUROPEAN)											
Mustard Pot w/lid	120										
PATRICIAN											
Candlesticks, pair	400										
PEACE											
Oil Lamp, 16", very rare		8500									
PEACH (NORTHWOOD)											
Bowl, 5"									50		
Bowl, 9"									150		
Butter									275		
Creamer, Sugar, or Spooner, each	400								150		
Pitcher				1300					950		
Tumbler	2000			150					175		
PEACH AND PEAR (DUGAN)											
Banana Bowl	90	150		600							
PEACH BLOSSOM											
Bowl, 7½"	60	75									
PEACHES											
Wine Bottle	45										
PEACOCK (MILLERSBURG)											
Banana Bowl, rare		3500									10000 V
Bowl, 5"	250	185	250	2500							
Bowl, square, sauce, rare	1000	1200									
Bowl, 9"	325	475	550								650 CM
Bowl, variant, 6", rare		175									
Bowl, shotgun, 7½", rare	500	500	450								
Bowl, square, 9", rare			2500								
Bowl, tricorner, very rare		4500									
Ice Cream Bowl, 5"	225	300	400								
Ice Cream Bowl, 10", scarce	3300	2400	3000								
Plate, 6", rare	1000	1350									
Proof Whimsey, rare	300	325	350								
Rose Bowl Whimsey, rare		4600									
Spittoon Whimsey, rare	6000	7500									10500 V
PEACOCK AND DAHLIA (FENTON)											
Bowl, 7½"	45	300	150	125							160 AQ
Plate, 8½", rare	450			600							
PEACOCK AND GRAPE (FENTON)											
Bowl, flat, 8" – 9"	60	175	200	300						1100	175 V
Bowl, footed, 8" – 9"	65	175	150	100						950	325 V
Plate, flat, 9" – 9½"	650	800	2700	1300							275 TL

Pattern Name	M	A	G	B	PO	AO	IB	IG	W	Red	Other
Plate, footed, 9"	300		425	475							300 LV
Nut Bowl, footed, scarce	55			125							
PEACOCK AND URN (FENTON)											
Bowl, 8½"	125	225	300	225					165	6000	1400 PeB
Compote	35	175	200	75					200		550 OG
Goblet, scarce	65	325	350	200					125		
Plate, 9", scarce	750	1800	900	1600					400		
PEACOCK AND URN (NORTHWOOD)											
Bowl, small, ruffled	75	100									
Bowl, large, ruffled	375	525	900								
Bowl, ice cream, 6"	125	100	675	115		2300	250	400	100		1300 ReB
Bowl, ice cream, 10"	550	600	2600	1200		31000	1050	1650	475		23000 SA
Plate, 6", rare	550	800		1300							
Plate, 11", rare	2200	2000						12000	13000		
(Add 25% for stippled)											
PEACOCK AND URN AND VARIANTS (MILLERSBURG)											
Banana Bowl, rare											11000 V
Bowl, ruffled, 6"	200	250	250								
Bowl, 9½"	350	400	425	2500							
Bowl, ice cream, 6", rare	300	150	300	800							
Bowl, ice cream, 10", rare	400	800	1200	4000							
Bowl, three in one, 10", rare				5000							
Compote, large, rare	1400	1600	2200								
Plate, 6", very rare	2300										
Plate, 10½", rare	3000										
Mystery Bowl, variant, 8½", rare	400	500	550	1850							
PEACOCK AT THE FOUNTAIN (DUGAN)											
Pitcher				525							
Tumbler		90		50							
PEACOCK AT THE FOUNTAIN (NORTHWOOD)											
Bowl, 5"	45	60	95	75			75	110	100		
Bowl, 9"	150	125	350	300			650	1250	300		
Butter	250	350	600	300			1200		625		
Compote, scarce	650	750	1800	975		3250	1500	1250	400		
Creamer or Spooner	135	120	300	200			250	300	150		
Creamer Whimsey, from punch cup, very rare				1200							
Orange Bowl, footed	275	900	3500	1200		12000					8000 SA
Punch Bowl w/base	500	1000		1000		36000	7500	8000			5500 LG
Punch Cup	30	50		60		1800	100	300	75		
Punch Cup Whimsey, rare		2000									
Pitcher	325	500	3500	475			2500		725		
Tumbler	35	55	300	45			145		200		800 PL
Spittoon Whimsey, rare		15000	17000								
Sugar	125	200	400	275			500		225		
PEACOCK GARDEN (NORTHWOOD)											
Vase, 8", very rare	16000										5000 WO
PEACOCK HEAD											
Tumbler, rare	150										
PEACOCK LAMP											
Carnival Base	800	450	500						500	900	
PEACOCKS (ON FENCE) (NORTHWOOD)											
Bowl, 8¾"	300	500	1300	600		1300	1400	1600	700		3000 EmG
Plate, 9"	500	775	1400	1500			1600	500	425		4500 CM
(Add 25% for stippled pieces)											
(Add 10% for pie crust edge bowls)											
PEACOCK TAIL (FENTON)											
Bonbon, handled, stemmed or flat	60	75	90	65							
Bowl, 5" – 7", various shapes	40	50	60	55	400					2500	
Bowl, 8" – 10", scarce	85	125	135	170							
Chop Plate, 11", rare	2200										
Compote	35	45	60	50					55		
Hat	30	40	55	50							
Hat, advertising	50		100								
Plate, 6" – 7"	900	800	900	1000							
Plate, 9"	900			600							
Spittoon Whimsey, very rare				4500							
PEACOCK TAIL (MILLERSBURG)											
Bowl, 9", very rare			400								
PEACOCK TAIL AND DAISY (WESTMORELAND)											
Bowl, very rare	1500	1900			2200 BO						
PEACOCK TAIL VARIANT (MILLERSBURG)											
Compote, scarce	70	150	175								
PEACOCK TREE *AKA: MAYURI (INDIA)											
Vase, 6"	165										
PEARL AND JEWELS (FENTON)											
Basket, 4"									200		
PEARL LADY (NORTHWOOD)											
Shade											90 IM

Pattern Name	M	A	G	B	PO	AO	IB	IG	W	Red	Other
PEARL #37 (NORTHWOOD)											
Shade					100						
PEARLY DOTS (WESTMORELAND)											
Bowl	40	60	70					250			40 TL
Compote	60				150						350 BO
Rose Bowl	40	75	60								300 TL
PEBBLE AND FAN (CZECH)											
Vase, 11¼", rare	375			775							900 V
PEBBLES (FENTON)											
Bonbon	25	45	65	50							
Bowl, sauce	15		30								
PENNY AND GENTLES											
Advertising Bowl, 6", rare		3000									
PENNY MATCH HOLDER (DUGAN)											
Match Holder, rare		1200									
PEOPLE'S VASE (MILLERSBURG)											
Vase, large, either shape, very rare	75000	65000	85000	100000							
PEPPER PLANT (FENTON)											
Hat Shape	40	85	100	60						725	
Advertising, General Furniture, rare		300									125 V
PERFECTION (MILLERSBURG)											
Pitcher, rare	5000	5500	6000								
Tumbler, rare	800	600	400								
PERIWINKLE (NORTHWOOD)											
Pitcher, two styles	450										
Tumbler, two styles	55										
PERSIAN GARDEN, (DUGAN)											
Bowl, berry, 5"	50	60			80				60		
Bowl, berry, 10"	235	325	1350		350				200		
Bowl, ice cream, 6"	70	125			100				75		
Bowl, ice cream, 11"	300	800			450				250		
Fruit Bowl w/base	675	650		4500	500				400		
Plate, 6", scarce	100	700		900	325				350		
Plate, chop, 13", scarce		12000			6000				3000		700 LV
Punch Bowl and Base, rare	1200	1650									2000 LV
(Add 25% for Pool of Pearls exterior)											
PERSIAN MEDALLION (FENTON)											
Bonbon	70	110	170	125						650	200 V
Bowl, 5"	40	60	45	50						1000	110 AQ
Bowl, 8½" – 9"	70	155	175	175						2800	1200 AM
Bowl, 9½", footed, plain exterior, very rare				2150							
Bowl, 10"	80	275	425	550							
Bowl, footed, small, w/Grape and Cable exterior, scarce	125										
Bowl, footed, large, w/Grape and Cable exterior, scarce	225	350	600	425				3500			
Compote, small	85	250	425	225					400		
Compote, large	90	375	325	100					225		200 CM
Fruit Bowl	150	300	325	225							
Hair Receiver	70	95		85					125		
Orange Bowl, footed	275	425	325	350							
Plate, 6"	160	300	450	350							
Plate, 7"	100	400	400	375							235 BA
Plate, 9½"	2000	3000	3500	800							300 BA
Plate, 9¼", two sides up, very rare	2300*								2700		
Plate, 10¾", chop plate, scarce				350							
Punch Bowl w/base	300	500	625	800							
Punch Cup	25	40	50	50							
Rose Bowl	75	325	300	400					210		
Spittoon Whimsey, very rare			7500								
(*Small plates w/Orange Tree exterior, add 25%)											
PERUVIAN PISCO INCA BOTTLE											
Figural Bottle, scarce											300 AM
PERUVIAN RINGS (ARGENTINA)											
Pitcher											500 TL
Tumbler											85 TL
PETAL AND FAN (DUGAN)											
Bowl, 5½" – 6"	40	80			125				95		
Bowl, mold proof, very scarce		125									
Bowl, 8" – 9"	85	250			150				225		
Bowl, 10" – 11"	140	325			250				300		
Plate, ruffled, 6"		550									
PETALED FLOWER											
*Interior of Leaf and Beads											
PETALS (DUGAN)											
Banana Bowl		90			100						
Bowl, 8¼"	40	50			80						
PETALS (NORTHWOOD)											
Compote	50	65	150	1100			925				
PETALS AND PRISMS (ENGLISH)											
Bowl, 9"	60										
Fruit Bowl, two pieces	90										

Pattern Name	M	A	G	B	PO	AO	IB	IG	W	Red	Other
Open Sugar	65										
Sugar, footed, 5"	70										
PETER RABBIT (FENTON)											
Bowl, 8½", very scarce	1250		2300	2000							2200 AM
Plate, 9½", rare	4000		6300	6000							
PHLOX (NORTHWOOD)											
Pitcher	400										
Tumbler	55										
PICKLE											
Paperweight, 4½"		75									
PIGEON											
Paperweight	200										
PILLAR AND DRAPE											
Shade					75 MO				90	625	
PILLAR AND SUNBURST (WESTMORELAND)											
Bowl, 7½"–8", ruffled or ice cream shape	20	35			70						80 AM
Plate, 8", very rare	200										
PILLAR FLUTE (IMPERIAL)											
Celery Vase	60	90									85 SM
Compote	50										225 BA
Creamer or Sugar	35										40 SM
Pickle Dish	30										35 CM
Rose Bowl	65										80 SM
PINCHED RIB											
Vase	85				180						
PINCHED SWIRL (DUGAN)											
Rose Bowl	100				135						
Spittoon Whimsey	150				200						
Vase	60				80						
PINEAPPLE (ENGLISH)											
Bowl, 4"	40										
Bowl, 7"	60	70		70							
Butter	85										
Compote	50	70		60							
Creamer	75	100									100 AQ
Rose Bowl	250										
Sugar, stemmed or flat	75										
PINEAPPLE AND FAN											
Tumble-up Set, three pieces	450			600							
Wine Set, complete, eight pieces	575										
PINEAPPLE CROWN											
Oval Bowl, 8"	60										
PINE CONE (FENTON)											
Bowl, 6"	45	80	150	65					265		200 SA
Bowl, ice cream shape, 6½", scarce	75	100	185	85							
Plate, 6¼"	135	325	375	250							
Plate, 6¼", 12 sided, smooth edge				350							
Plate, 7½"	450	550		375							1000 AM
PINNACLE (JAIN)											
Tumbler	200										
Vase	350			500							
PIN-UPS, (AUSTRALIAN)											
Bowl, 4"–6", rare	95	175									
Bowl, 7"–8¼", rare	200	450									
PINWHEEL (ENGLISH)											
Bowl, 6", scarce	75										
Rose Bowl, 5½", rare	250										
PINWHEEL-DERBY (ENGLISH)											
Bowl, 8", rare	125										
Vase, 6½", rare	350	450									
Vase, 8", rare	200	375		450							
PIPE CANDY CONTAINER											
One Shape									200		
PIPE HOLDER ASHTRAY											
Ashtray	200										
PIPE HUMIDOR (MILLERSBURG)											
Tobacco Jar w/lid, very rare	13000	10000	11000								
PIPE MATCH HOLDER											
One Shape	100										
PLAID (FENTON)											
Bowl, 8¾"	200	350	425	350						2300	425 LV
Plate, 9", rare	400	900		575						8000	
PLAIN AND FANCY (HEISEY)											
Pitcher, very scarce	450										
Tumbler, very scarce	125										
PLAIN COIN DOT (FENTON)											
Rose Bowl	65										
PLAIN JANE											
Paperweight	90										
PLAIN JANE (IMPERIAL)											
Basket	30	125							200		65 SM
Bowl, 4"	15	50	35								25 SM
Bowl, 4", smooth edge	25										55 PB
Bowl, 8"–9"	40	70	45								65 SM
Bowl, 10"–12"	60	100	70								100 SM

Pattern Name	M	A	G	B	PO	AO	IB	IG	W	Red	Other
Rose Bowl, small	45										75 SM
PLAIN PETALS (NORTHWOOD)											
Nappy, scarce		85	90								
Interior of Leaf and Beads nappy											
PLAIN PILSNER											
Stemmed Glass, 6"	25										
PLAIN RAYS											
Bowl, 9"	40	45	50	65							
Compote	45	55	60	70							
PLEATS											
Bowl	55										
Rose Bowl	95										
PLEATS AND HEARTS											
Shade											90 PM
PLUME PANELS (FENTON)											
Vase, 7" – 12"	30	100	225	165						1300	500 V
Vase, JIP, rare										1400	
PLUME PANELS AND BOWS											
Tumbler, scarce	150										
PLUMS AND CHERRIES (NORTHWOOD)											
Spooner, rare				1800							
Sugar, rare				1800							
Tumbler, very rare	2500			4000							
PLUTEC (MCKEE)											
Vase	200										
POINSETTIA (IMPERIAL)											
Milk Pitcher	95	2500	500								300 SM
POINSETTIA (NORTHWOOD)											
Bowl, 8½" – 9½"	400	475	8000	600		11000	1800		8500		350 SM
POLO											
Ashtray	85										
POMONE (CRISTALERIAS PICCARDO)											
Candy Dish, covered											250 AM
POMPEIAN (DUGAN)											
Hyacinth Vase	70				175				250		
Vase Whimsey, pinched three sides	110	225			300						
POND LILY (FENTON)											
Bonbon	55	125	125	60					150		600 PeB
PONY (DUGAN)											
Bowl, 8½"	90	250						1100			1400 AQ
Plate (age questionable), 9", rare	450	700									
POODLE											
Powder Jar w/lid	20										
POOL OF PEARLS											
Exterior only											
POPPY (MILLERSBURG)											
Compote, scarce	575	725	750								
Salver, rare	2000	1700	1600								
POPPY (NORTHWOOD)											
Pickle Dish, oval	125	250	325	350		2000	600		325		700 AQ
Tray, oval, rare		325		450							
POPPY AND HOBSTAR											
Butter											165 AM
POPPY AND FISH NET (IMPERIAL)											
Vase, 6", rare										750	
POPPY SCROLL (NORTHWOOD)											
Bowl, 11", rare	1800						3600				
(AKA: Oriental Poppy)											
POPPY SCROLL VARIANT (NORTHWOOD)											
Compote, 7½"											150 V
POPPY SHOW (NORTHWOOD)											
Bowl, 8½"	425	550	2200	2200		20000	1400	1200	400		1000 LG
Plate, 9", scarce	850	1400	3500	3600		26000	1650	2200	575		
POPPY SHOW VASE (IMPERIAL)											
Hurricane Whimsey		2500							2500		
Lamp Whimsey	1400	1400									
Vase, 12", old only	700	3500	1100								1300 SM
POPPY VARIANT (NORTHWOOD)											
Bowl, 7" – 8"	40	60	70	175	350	595					85 ALS
POPPY VARIANT BASE											
Bowl, 7" – 8", very scarce	60	75	95								
POPPY WREATH											
Amaryllis exterior											
PORTLAND (U.S. GLASS)											
Bowl, 5"	95										
Bowl, 8"	170										
Toothpick Holder	140										
Wine	165										
PORTLAND ELKS BELL (FENTON)											
1912 Portland Bell, very rare				24500							
PORTLY (FENTON)											
Candlesticks, pair									85		
POST LANTERN											
Shade											95 AM

Pattern Name	M	A	G	B	PO	AO	IB	IG	W	Red	Other
POTPOURRI (MILLERSBURG)											
Milk Pitcher, rare	2500	4500									
POWDER HORN (CAMBRIDGE)											
Candy Holder	200										
PRAYER RUG (FENTON)											
Bonbon, scarce											1500 IC
Creamer, very rare											3300 IC
Plate, 7", very rare											7000 IC
PREMIUM (IMPERIAL)											
Candlesticks, pair	45	175								425	175 SM
PREMIUM SWIRL (IMPERIAL)											
Candlesticks, pair	50										200 SM
PRESCUT (MCKEE)											
Vase											150 CM
PRESSED HEXAGON (MCKEE)											
Covered Butter	150										
Creamer, Sugar, or Spooner, each	85										
PRETTY PANELS (FENTON)											
Pitcher w/lid										500	
Tumbler, handled	60							90			
PRETTY PANELS (NORTHWOOD)											
Pitcher	125		150								
Tumbler	60		70								
PRIMROSE (MILLERSBURG)											
Bowl, ruffled, 8¾"	100	225	200	4500							175 CM
Bowl, ice cream shape, scarce	135	250	225								
Bowl, goofus exterior, rare	900										
PRIMROSE AND FISHNET (IMPERIAL)											
Vase, 6", rare										750	
PRIMROSE AND RIBBON											
Lightshade	90										
PRIMROSE PANELS (IMPERIAL)											
Shade	60										
PRINCELY PLUMES											
Caster, 3¼"		475									
PRINCESS (U.S. GLASS)											
Lamp, complete, rare		950									
PRINCESS FEATHER (WESTMORELAND)											
Compote	85										
PRINCETON (CZECH)											
Vase, 10½", rare	750										
PRISCILLA											
Spooner	75										
PRISM											
Shakers, pair	60										
Tray, 3"	50										
PRISM AND CANE (ENGLISH)											
Bowl, 5", rare	45	65									
PRISM AND DAISY BAND (IMPERIAL)											
Bowl, 5"	15										
Bowl, 8"	25										
Compote	35										
Creamer or Sugar, each	30										
Vase	25										
PRISM AND FAN (DAVISON)											
Basket, handled	150										
PRISM AND PLEATS											
Bowl, 8½"	45										
Rose Bowl	70										
PRISM AND STAR											
Shot Glass, 2¼"	75										
PRISM BAND (FENTON)											
Pitcher	200			300				450			
Tumbler	30			45				100			
PRISM COLUMNS											
Bowl, low, 7¾"	55										
Rose Bowl	75										
PRISM PANELS											
Bowl, 8" – 9"	60										
PRISMS (WESTMORELAND)											
Compote, 5", scarce	50	90	100								150 TL
Nappy, one handled, rare			375								
PRISM WITH BLOCK (WESTMORELAND)											
Creamer	95										
PRIYA (INDIA)											
Tumbler	135										
PROPELLER (IMPERIAL)											
Bowl, 9½", rare	175										
Compote	50		85								80 SM
Vase, stemmed, rare	90										
PROUD PUSS (CAMBRIDGE)											
Bottle	85										

72

Pattern Name	M	A	G	B	PO	AO	IB	IG	W	Red	Other
PROVENCE											
Pitcher, rare	800										
Tumbler	150										
*AKA: Bars and Cross Box											
PULLED LOOP (DUGAN)											
Vase, squat, 5" – 7"	80	175			300				385		750 CeB
Vase, 8" – 16"	40	75	300	175	250						950 CeB
PUMP, HOBNAIL (NORTHWOOD)											
One shape (age questionable)		850									
PUPPY											
Mini Candy Holder	100										
PURITAN (MCKEE)											
Bowl, 4", rare				250							
Plate, 6", rare	150										
PUZZLE (DUGAN)											
Bonbon or Compote	40	85	150	130	85				125		165 LV
PUZZLE PIECE											
One Shape				100							
QUARTER BLOCK											
Butter	125										
Creamer or Sugar, each	60										
QUATREFOIL BAND											
Shot Glass, enameled	45										
QUEEN'S JEWEL											
Goblet	55										
QUEEN'S LAMP											
Lamp, complete, rare			3000								
QUESTION MARKS (DUGAN)											
Bonbon	25	40		225	50			300	60		80 LV
Cake Plate, stemmed, rare	155	250							200		
Compote	40	70			125				75		70 BA
(Add 50% for exterior pattern)											
QUILL (DUGAN)											
Pitcher, rare	900	2000									
Tumbler, rare	200	250									
QUINCY JEWELRY (FENTON)											
Hat, scarce			225								
QUILTED DIAMOND (IMPERIAL)											
Exterior pattern to some Imperial Pansy pieces. Priced under Pansy											
QUILTED ROSE (EDA)											
Bowl, 5½"	50										
Bowl, 8"	125										
QUORN MUG											
Mug w/lettering	100										
RABBIT BANK											
Small	90										
Large	100										
RADIANCE (NEW MARTINSVILLE)											
Vase, 12", very rare	400										
RADIANCE (RIVERSIDE)											
Bowl, 5"	25										
Bowl, 8"	85										
Butter	150										
Compote, open	150										
Compote, covered	175										
Creamer or Spooner	100										
Jelly Compote	125										
Mustard Jar, covered	175										
Goblet	125										
Shakers, each	55										
Sugar	125										
Syrup	325										
Toothpick Holder	85										
Pitcher	225										
Tumbler	70										
RAGGED ROBIN (FENTON)											
Bowl, 8¾", scarce	85	150	150	125							
RAINBOW (MCKEE)											
Whiskey Glass, scarce	125										
RAINBOW (NORTHWOOD)											
Bowl, 8"	45	65	75								125 LV
Compote	45	65	80								
Plate, 9", scarce		100	150								
Plate, handgrip, 9", scarce		150	175								
RAINBOW OPAQUE (NORTHWOOD)											
Bowls, various											30 – 75 OB
RAINBOW VARIANT (NORTHWOOD)											
Compote, small			65								
RAINDROPS (DUGAN)											
Banana Bowl, 9¾"		185			250						
Bowl, 9"	65	150			200						
Nut Bowl Whimsey					275						
RAMBLER ROSE (DUGAN)											
Pitcher	160	250		400							

Pattern Name	M	A	G	B	PO	AO	IB	IG	W	Red	Other
Tumbler	30	50		65							
RANGER (IMPERIAL)											
Bowl, round, 4½" – 8"	25										
Bowl, flared, 6¼" – 10"	40										60 CM
Breakfast Set, two pieces	90										
Cracker Jar	80										
Nappy	45										
Pitcher	450										
Tumbler	150										
Sherbet, footed	55										
Vase, 8"	95										145 CM
RANGER (MEXICAN)											
Butter	150										
Creamer	40										
Decanter w/stopper, scarce	225										
Milk Pitcher	150										
Perfume, 5¼"	150										
Shot Glass, rare	450										
Sugar	75										
RANGER (EUROPEAN)											
Tumbler	100										
RANGER (ENGLISH)											
Toothpick Holder	100										
Vase, 10"	65										
RASPBERRY (NORTHWOOD)											
Gravy Boat, footed	85	135	200	300							400 TL
Milk Pitcher	175	275	325				2200	2400	1000		3550 LG
Pitcher	200	325	400	10000			1250	5000	850		
Tumbler	75	60	100	950			250	375			85 HO
RATH'S RINGS											
Cracker Jar	125										
RAYS (DUGAN)											
Bowl, 5"	40	50	50		70						
Bowl, 9"	55	90	90		125						
Plate, 6¼", very scarce		190									
RAYS AND RIBBON (MILLERSBURG)											
Banana Bowl, rare		1400	1250								
Bowl, round or ruffled, 8½" – 9½"	175	225	225	3600							
Bowl, tricornered	210	275	325								11000 V
Bowl, square, scarce	325	600	600								14000 V
Chop Plate, rare "			900								
Rose Bowl, rare	900	950									
RED PANELS (IMPERIAL)											
Shade										225	
REGAL (NORTHWOOD)											
Bowl, Sauce, 4½", rare					250						
REGAL											
Jardiniere	275										
REGAL CANE											
Cordial	200										
Decanter w/ stopper	600										
Goblet	200										
Pitcher	650										
Tray	300										
Tumbler, very rare	1500										
REGAL CANE MINIATURE											
Child's Mug	100										
REGAL FLOWER (DUGAN/DIAMOND)											
Vase, decorated, 14", rare	350										
REGAL IRIS (CONSOLIDATED)											
Gone with the Wind Lamp, rare	2500									12000	
REGAL ROSE (IMPERIAL)											
Vase, rare		300									
REGAL SWIRL											
Candlestick, each	75										
REICHEL'S ROSES											
Bowl, small footed, rare	150										
REKORD (EDA)											
Bowl				125							
Vase				300							
REINDEER (GERMANY)											
Tumbler	300										
REKORD (EDA)											
Vase, rare				425							
Bowl, scarce				225							
REVERSE DRAPERY WITH LEAVES											
Oil Lamp, rare	400										
REX											
Buttermilk Pitcher	75										
Pitcher	50										
Tumbler	10										
REX (EDA)											
Vase	275			550							475 MMG
RIB AND FLUTE											
Vase, 12¼", very scarce	125										

Pattern Name	M	A	G	B	PO	AO	IB	IG	W	Red	Other
RIB AND PANEL											
Spittoon Whimsey	200										
Vase	125	300		300	400						
RIBBED BAND AND SCALES											
Pitcher	200										
Tumbler	65										
RIBBED BEADED SPEARS (JAIN)											
Tumbler	150										
RIBBED ELLIPSE (HIGBEE)											
Mug, rare											150 HA
Tumbler	250										
RIBBED PANELS											
Mustard Pot	350										
Shot Glass	225										
Toothpick Holder	300										
RIBBED SWIRL											
Pitcher	125		225								
Tumbler	60		80								
RIBBED TORNADO											
See Tornado (Northwood)											
RIBBON AND BLOCK											
Lamp, compote	600										
RIBBON AND FERN											
Atomizer, 7"	90										
RIBBONS AND LEAVES (ENGLISH)											
Sugar, open	55										
RIBBON SWIRL											
Cake Stand, very scarce											425 AM
RIBBON TIE (FENTON)											
Bowl, 8¼"	110	275	300	145							
Plate, 9½", low ruffled		250		325						5600	
RIBS (SMALL BASKET) (CZECHOSLOVAKIA)										7500	
Bud Vase	60										
Perfume	110										
Pin Box	75										
Puff Box	95										
Ring Tree	60										
Soap Dish	60										
Tumbler	85										
RIIHIMAKI (RIIHIMAKI)											
Tumbler				225							
RIIHIMAKI STAR											
Ashtray, very scarce	150			275							
RINDSKOPF											
Vase, 5¾"	150										
RINGED SHAKERS											
Shaker, each, either top	25			40							35 CRAN
RINGS (HOCKING)											
Vase, 8"	25										
RIPPLE (IMPERIAL)											
Vase, squat, 4" – 7"	150	175	100								150 SM
Vase, standard, 7" – 12"	40	145	110	600					200	1500	145 TL
Vase, mid-size, 12" – 15"	200	275	200								265 SM
Vase, funeral, 15" – 21"	175	450	400								500 TL
RISING COMET (AKA: COMET)											
Vase, 6" – 10"	150 – 400										
RISING SUN (U.S. GLASS)											
Bowl, small sauce	35										
Butter Dish	400										
Creamer	75										
Juice Tumbler, rare	150										
Pitcher, two shapes, very scarce	325			1400							
Pitcher, squat, rare	600										
Tumbler, scarce	135			350							
Sugar	95										
Tray, rare	300			500							
RIVER GLASS											
Bowl, 8" – 9"	65										
Celery Vase	85										
RIVERSIDE'S FLORENTINE											
Bowl, small	20										
Bowl, large	55										
ROARING TWENTIES (CAMBRIDGE)											
Powder Jar	180										
ROBIN (IMPERIAL)											
Mug, old only	60										150 SM
Pitcher, old only, scarce	150										650 SM
Tumbler, old only, scarce	35										75 SM
ROCK CRYSTAL (MCKEE)											
Punch Bowl w/base, rare		800									
Punch Cup, rare		75									
ROCOCO (IMPERIAL)											
Bowl, 5", footed	40										225 LV
Bowl, 9", footed, rare	175										
Vase, 5½"	125										200 SM

Pattern Name	M	A	G	B	PO	AO	IB	IG	W	Red	Other
ROLL											
Cordial Set, complete (decanter, stopper, and six glasses)	350										
Pitcher, rare											300 CL
Tumbler, scarce	40										
Shakers, each, rare	45										
ROLLED BAND (CZECH)											
Pitcher	125										
Tumbler	30										
ROLLED RIBS (NEW MARTINSVILLE)											
Bowl, 8" – 10"											200 MMG
ROLLED RIM MINI BOWL											
Bowl, 3½"	50										
ROLLING RIDGES											
Tumbler	25										
ROLY POLY											
Jar w/lid	30										
ROMAN ROSETTE (U.S. GLASS)											
Goblet, 6", rare											110 CL
ROOD'S CHOCOLATES (FENTON)											
Plate, advertising		3600									
ROOSTER											
Novelty Ashtray, rare	325										
ROSALIND (MILLERSBURG)											
Bowl, 5", rare	1300	300	550								
Bowl, 10", scarce	200	250	275								600 AQ
Compote (variant), 6", rare		675	575								
Compote, ruffled, 8", rare	2500										
Compote, jelly, 9", rare	4000	3800	4000	15000							
Chop Plate, 11", very rare	10000										
Plate, 9", very rare		2400	3000								
ROSE											
Bottle									125		
ROSE AND FISHNET											
Vase, very scarce									750		
ROSE ANN											
Shade	40										
ROSE BAND											
Tumbler, rare	700										
ROSE BOUQUET											
Bonbon, rare									400		
ROSE COLUMN (MILLERSBURG)											
Vase, rare	5500	5500	3800	10000							6000 TL
Vase, experimental, very rare		21000									
ROSE GARDEN (SWEDEN AND GERMAN)											
Bowl, 6", scarce	75	175		125							
Bowl, 8¼"	75	300		150							
Butter, rare	300			450							
Pitcher, rare	800			1100							
Rose Bowl, small, very scarce	500										
Rose Bowl, large, very scarce				600							
Vase, round, rare	425			750							
Vase, small, scarce	325			425							
Vase, medium, scarce	425			950							
Vase, large, scarce	1000			900							
ROSE IN SWIRL											
Vase	75										
ROSE PANELS (AUSTRALIAN)											
Compote, large	175										
ROSE PINWHEEL											
Bowl, rare	1600	1900	2000								
ROSE POWDER JAR											
Jar w/lid	100										
ROSES AND FRUIT (MILLERSBURG)											
Bonbon, footed, rare	600	800	800	3000							
ROSES AND GREEK KEY											
Plate, square, very rare	7500										21000 SM
ROSES AND RUFFLES (CONSOLIDATED GLASS)											
Lamp, Gone with the Wind, rare	2900								10000		
ROSE SHOW (NORTHWOOD)											
Bowl, 8¾"	375	650	1600	725		1800	1000	1700			900 AQ
Plate, 9½"	725	1200	2500	950		10000	2000	2900	525		8000 IGO
ROSE SHOW VARIANT (NORTHWOOD)											
Bowl, 8¾"	900			1300							1200 ReB
Plate, 9"	1550			1400							2400 ReB
ROSE SPRAY (FENTON)											
Compote	50						145	145	125		
ROSE SPRIG											
Mini Loving Cup	195										
ROSETIME											
Vase, 7½"	100										
ROSE TREE (FENTON)											
Bowl, 10", very rare	2000			3300							

Pattern Name	M	A	G	B	PO	AO	IB	IG	W	Red	Other
ROSETTE (NORTHWOOD)											
Bowl, footed, 7" – 9"	60	100	165								
ROSE WINDOWS											
Pitcher, very rare	900										
Tumbler, rare	200										
Tumbler, advertising, very rare	550										
ROUND ROBIN											
Bowl, small berry	10										
Cup	10										
Creamer	15										
Plate, 6" – 8"	15										
Plate, chop size, 12"	20										
Saucer	10										
Sherbet, footed	10	65									
Sugar	20										
ROUND UP (DUGAN)											
Bowl, 8¾"	150	400		300	250				195		600 LV
Plate, 9"	250	525		475	600				350		
ROW BOAT											
Novelty Boat	75										
ROYAL DIAMONDS											
Tumbler, rare	150										
ROYAL GARLAND (JAIN)											
Tumbler	200										
ROYAL PINEAPPLE											
Vase	80										
ROYAL SWANS (SOWERBY)											
Vase, rare	1500	2000									
ROYALTY (IMPERIAL)											
Fruit Bowl w/stand	100										100 SM
Punch Bowl w/base	150										
Punch Cup	35										
RUFFLED MINI CUP AND SAUCER											
Cup and Saucer, miniature	100										
RUFFLED RIB											
Spittoon, either top shape	65	80	70		800						
RUFFLES AND RINGS (NORTHWOOD)											
Bowl, 8½", scarce	125	150			500						
Exterior pattern											
RUFFLES AND RINGS WITH DAISY BAND (NORTHWOOD)											
Bowl, footed, 8½", rare					1100 MO						
RUSTIC (FENTON)											
Vase, squat, 6" – 7½" (3"+ base)	50	80	85	80							
Vase, standard, 8" – 13" (3"+ base)	35	70	65	65	1400				125	3500	1200 LO
Vase, midsize, 11" – 17" (4"+ base)	75	145	135	125					200		
Vase, funeral, 16" – 23" (5"+ base)	1900	2000	2300	1800					950		15000 EmG
Whimsey Pinched Jardiniere, very rare				2500							
Vase Oddity, with penny in base		1000									
Vase Whimsey, spittoon shape, very rare		7500									
Variant Vase *(10% more than above prices of regular vases)											
(*Add $1000 for funeral size with banded plunger base)											
RUTH PARLOR ASHTRAY											
Ashtray, three pieces, 22" tall, rare	400										
SACIC ASHTRAY (ARGENTINA)											
Ashtray	95										
SACIC BOTTLE (ARGENTINA)											
Soda Bottle, very scarce	75										
SAILBOAT (FENTON)											
Bowl, 6"	40	75	125	70					600		275 V
Compote	65			195							
Goblet	225	400	500	100							190 PB
Plate, 6"	350			850					1000		250 LV
Wine	35			80							350 V
Wine (variant), scarce	55			125							
SAILING SHIP (BELMONT)											
Plate, 8"	25										
SAINT (ENGLISH)											
Candlesticks, each	300										
SALT CUP (VARIOUS MAKERS)											
One Shape, averaged	50	60	90								85 V
SANSARA (JAIN)											
Tumbler	150										
SAN TELMOS											
Ashtray	75										
SARITA *AKA: ANNA EVE (INDIA)											
Tumbler	200										
SATIN SWIRL											
Atomizer											75 CL
SAVANNA'S LILY											
Single Lily on metal stand	275										
SAWTOOTH BAND											
Tumbler, rare	250										

Pattern Name	M	A	G	B	PO	AO	IB	IG	W	Red	Other
Pitcher	375										
SAWTOOTHED HONEYCOMB (UNION GLASS)											
Pickle Dish, 7½"	85										
SAWTOOTH PRISMS											
Jelly Jar, three sizes	60										
SCALE BAND (FENTON)											
Bowl, 6"	25			100					90	325	
Bowl, 8½" – 10", very scarce	100			400							350 V
Plate, flat, 6½"	50									425	
Plate, dome base, 7"	80									600	
Pitcher	150		800	550							350 V
Tumbler	40		225	300							
SCALES (WESTMORELAND)											
Bonbon	40	50			100	200 BO					75 TL
Bowl, deep, 5"		40									
Bowl, 7" – 10"					90 IM	225 BO					100 PeB
Plate, 6"	45	65									65 TL
Plate, 9"		100				250 BO					200 MMG
SCARAB PAPERWEIGHT											
Paperweight, large, 6" – 7"		475									
SCEPTER											
Candleholder, pair, scarce	95										125 SM
SCOTCH THISTLE (FENTON)											
Compote	50	80	90	75							
SCOTTIE											
Paperweight, rare	200										
Powder Jar w/lid	20										
SCROLL (WESTMORELAND)											
Pin Tray	75										
SCROLL AND FLOWER PANELS (IMPERIAL)											
Vase, 10", old only	600	2350									2000 SM
SCROLL AND GRAPE (MILLERSBURG)											
Punch Bowl w/base, very rare		5000									
Multi-Fruits and Flowers exterior											
SCROLL EMBOSSED (IMPERIAL)											
Bowl, 4" – 7"	40	65	185								100 SM
Bowl, 8" – 9"	50	135								1300	425 TL
Bowl Whimsey		175									
Compote, goblet shaped whimsey		400	225								
Compote, miniature	140	375									265 LV
Compote, small	40	115	55	750							150 AM
Compote, large, either exterior	45	125	85								165 AM
Dessert, stemmed	65	110	90								
Nut Bowl, scarce		175									
Plate, 9"	100	375	125								290 LV
(Add 10% for File exterior and 50% for Hobstar and Tassels exterior)											
SCROLL EMBOSSED VARIANT (ENGLISH)											
Ashtray, handled, 5"	45	60									
Plate, 7"	165										
SCROLL FLUTED (IMPERIAL)											
Rose Bowl, very rare	325										
SCROLL PANEL											
Lamp										475	
SEACOAST (MILLERSBURG)											
Pin Tray, very scarce	1000	800	800								900 CM
SEAFOAM (DUGAN)											
Exterior only											
SEAGULLS (CZECH)											
Vase, very rare	1000										1500 PB
SEAGULLS (DUGAN)											
Bowl, 6½", scarce	110										
SEAWEED											
Lamp, two sizes	250										
Lamp Variant, 8½", rare						400					
SEAWEED (MILLERSBURG)											
Bowl, 5" – 6½", rare	850	1000	2000	2800							
Bowl, 9", scarce	275	525	400	2000							
Bowl, 10½", ruffled or three in one, scarce	400	600	450								1750 AQ
Bowl, 6", ice cream shape, very rare				2000							
Bowl, ice cream, 10½", rare	500	1600	1900	5500							
Plate, 10", rare	1800	2500	3350								
SERPENTINE ROSE (ENGLISH)											
Rose Bowl, footed	90										
SERPENT VASE (JAIN)											
Vase, rare	500										
SERRATED FLUTE											
Vase, 8" – 13", scarce	30	100	75								40 CM
SERRATED RIBS											
Shakers, each	60										

Pattern Name	M	A	G	B	PO	AO	IB	IG	W	Red	Other
SHALIMAR (JAIN)											
Tumbler	150										
SHANGHI (CHINA)											
Tumbler, two kinds	50										
SHARON'S GARDEN											
Bowl					350						
SHARP											
Shot Glass	50										
SHASTA DAISY											
Pitcher	250							425	375		
Tumbler	35							55	40		
SHASTA DAISY W/PRISM BAND											
Tumbler	45							75	65		
SHAZAM (INDIA)											
Pitcher	425										
Tumbler	100										
SHELL											
Shade									75		
SHELL (IMPERIAL)											
Bowl, 7" – 9"	45	150	75								125 SM
Plate, 8½"	375	1000	600								500 SM
SHELL AND BALLS											
Perfume, 2½"	65										
SHELL AND JEWEL (WESTMORELAND)											
Creamer w/lid	55	65	60						90		
Sugar w/lid	55	65	60						90		
Sugar Whimsey (age ?)			200								
SHELL AND SAND (IMPERIAL)											
Bowl, 7" – 9"	125	250	100								225 SM
Plate, 9"	800	1500	275								900 SM
SHERATON (U.S. GLASS)											
Butter											130 PM
Creamer or Spooner											75 PM
Sugar											90 PM
Pitcher											170 PM
Tumbler											50 PM
SHIELDED FLOWER											
Tumbler	150										
SHIP'S DECANTER											
Decanter Set, complete	2000										
SHIP AND STARS											
Plate, 8"	25										
SHIRLEY'S SUNBURST											
Bowl, 6½", rare	250										
SHOE CANDY CONTAINER											
Novelty Candy Container									125		
SHOVEL											
Mini Novelty	250										
SHRIKE (AUSTRALIAN)											
Bowl, 5"	165	180									
Bowl, 9½"	350	600									
Whimsey Bowl, square, very rare		750									1200 AQ
SHRINE CHAMPAGNES (U.S. GLASS)											
New Orleans Champagne											100 CL
Pittsburgh/ Louisville Champagne, very scarce											200 CL
Rochester Champagne											100 CL
SHRINE SHEATH OF WHEAT											
Toothpick, St. Paul, Minnesota											75 CL
SIGNATURE (JEANNETTE)											
Open Candy	35										
Parfait, tall	25										
Sherbet	15										
SIGNET (ENGLISH)											
Sugar w/lid, 6½"	75										
SILVER AND GOLD											
Pitcher	150										
Tumbler	50										
SILVER OVERLAY CRUET											
Cruet, decorated with silver overlay											85 CRAN
SILVER QUEEN (FENTON)											
Pitcher	250										
Tumbler	60										
SIMPLE SIMON (NORTHWOOD)											
Vase	60	75	90								
SIMPLICITY SCROLL (WESTMORELAND)											
Toothpick Holder, two sizes											200–300 SM
SIMPLICE (ITALY)											
Lidded Jar with wire handles	90										
SINGING BIRDS (NORTHWOOD)											
Bowl, 5"	30	35	45	300							
Bowl, 10"	75	275	295	5500							
Butter	185	325	425								

79

Pattern Name	M	A	G	B	PO	AO	IB	IG	W	Red	Other
Creamer	75	85	125								
Mug	65	100	200	190		1200	435		600		200 LV
Mug, stippled	150	400	400	525							
Mug Whimsey w/spout, very rare	750										
Pitcher	350	500	1100								
Tumbler	45	70	90								
Sherbet, rare	400										
Spooner	75	125	150								
Sugar	175	250	300								
SINGLE FLOWER (DUGAN)											
Banana Bowl, 9½", rare					375						
Basket Whimsey, handled, rare	225				350						
Bowl, 8"	35	45	125		140						
Bowl, 9" (Lily of the Valley decoration)					100						
Hat	30	45	65								
SINGLE FLOWER FRAMED (DUGAN)											
Bowl, 5"	40	65			85						
Bowl, 8¾"	65	150	125		130						
Plate		300			250						
SIR LANCE											
Tumbler, rare	150										
SITTING BULLDOG PAPERWEIGHT											
One Shape	350										
SITTING DOG PAPERWEIGHT											
Novelty Paperweight	75										
SIX PANEL FLUTE											
Tumbler	20										
SIX PETALS (DUGAN)											
Bowl, 8½"	40	125	75	125	75				85		400 BA
Hat	45	70	85		100						150 BA
SIX RING											
Tumbler, three sizes	30 – 40										
SIX-SIDED (IMPERIAL)											
Candlestick, each	225	750	300								250 SM
SIX SIDED BLOCK											
Creamer, child's											55 LV
Sugar, child's											95 LV
SKATER'S SHOE (U.S. GLASS)											
One Shape	120										
SKI STAR (DUGAN)											
Banana Bowl		175			225						
Basket, handled, rare					500						
Bowl, 5"	40	65	75	100	85						
Bowl, 8" – 10"	60	250		250	200						
Plate, 6"					275						
Plate, handgrip, 8" – 10"					295						
Rose Bowl, rare					700						
SLEWED HORSESHOE											
Bowl, 8" – 9"				165							
Punch Cup											75 – G. Slag
SLICK WILLIE (HALE BATHS)											
Vase, 13"	125										
SLIM JIM											
Vase, 13"	45										
SLIPPER ROLLER SKATE											
Novelty Skate	90										
SMALL BASKET											
One Shape	50										
SMALL BLACKBERRY (NORTHWOOD)											
Compote	55	65	75								
SMALL PALMS											
Shade	45										
SMALL RIB											
Compote	40	45	50								60 AM
Rose Bowl, stemmed	50	65	80								75 AM
SMALL RIB AND VARIANT (FENTON)											
Card Tray Whimsey	40	60									
Compote, 4½"	30	50	50	55							
Compote, 5½"	35	55	55	60							
Spittoon Whimsey, stemmed, rare	100	150	150	170							200 AM
SMALL THUMBPRINT											
Creamer or Sugar	60										
Mug, scarce	100										
Toothpick Holder	70										
SMOOTHIE											
Vase				75							
SMOOTH PANELS (IMPERIAL)											
Bowl, 6½"	30										35 SM
Rose Bowl, scarce	50										75 SM
Sweet Pea Vase, scarce	75										60 CM
Vase, squat, 4" – 7"	50								100	250	300 MMG
Vase, standard, 8" – 14"	40	150	175		200					325	250 MMG
Vase, funeral, 15" – 18"	125									800	350 TL
SMOOTH PANELS CUT #90											
Vases, 5" – 7", very scarce	150										

Pattern Name	M	A	G	B	PO	AO	IB	IG	W	Red	Other
SMOOTH RAYS (DUGAN)											
Bowl	45	75			100						
SMOOTH RAYS (FENTON)											
Spittoon Whimsey, rare	450										
SMOOTH RAYS (IMPERIAL)											
Bowl, 9" – 10"	25										20 SM
Champagne	40										40 SM
Custard Cup	15										15 SM
Goblet, two sizes	30										30 SM
Plate, 8"	35										40 SM
Plate, 12"	50										55 SM
Pitcher	65										75 SM
Rose Bowl	80										
Tumbler	20										25 SM
Wine, two sizes	35										40 SM
SMOOTH RAYS (NORTHWOOD)											
Bonbon	35	45	55								
Bowl, 6" – 7"	30	40	45	750							60 ALS
Compote	40	45	55								
SMOOTH RAYS (WESTMORELAND)											
Bowl, flat, 6" – 9"	40	55	50		75	125 BO					75 TL
Bowl, dome base, 5" – 7½"			60		85	125 BO					75 TL
Compote	35	45	55		75						125 MMG
Plate, 7" – 9"	75	100	110								150 AM
Rose Bowl	40	70									85 AM
SNOW FANCY (IMPERIAL)											
Bowl, 5"			60								
Bowl, 8½", very scarce	235										
Creamer or Spooner	50										
SNOWFLAKE (CAMBRIDGE)											
Tankard, very rare	2000										
SODA GOLD (IMPERIAL)											
Bowl, 9"	45										55 SM
Candlestick, 3½", each	55										60 SM
Chop Plate, scarce	125										
Pitcher	200										350 SM
Tumbler	50										200 SM
Shakers, scarce	125										140 SM
SODA GOLD SPEARS (DUGAN)											
Bowl, 4½"	30										30 CL
Bowl, 8½"	40										40 CL
Plate, 9"	75										150 CL
SONGBIRD (JAIN)											
Tumbler, very scarce	225										
SONGBIRD PAPERWEIGHT											
Novelty Paperweight	85										
SOUR PUSS ASHTRAY											
Novelty Ashtray	200										
SOUTACHE (DUGAN)											
Bowl, 10", scarce					200						
Plate, 10½", rare					350						
Lamp, complete, scarce	350										
SOUTHERN IVY											
Wine, two sizes	45										
SOUVENIR BANDED											
Mug	85										
SOUVENIR BELL											
One Shape, lettering	180										
SOUVENIR MINIATURE											
One Shape, lettering	50										
SOUVENIR MUG (MCKEE)											
Any lettering	65										
SOUVENIR PIN TRAY (U.S. GLASS)											
One Size (same as Portland pattern)											75 PM
SOUVENIR VASE (U.S. GLASS)											
Vase, 6½", rare	100	135			150	400					
SOWERBY DRAPE											
Vase											225 BA
SOWERBY FLOWER BLOCK (ENGLISH)											
Flower Frog	60										
SOWERBY FROG											
Flower Frog, footed, scarce	125			200							225 BA
SOWERBY SWAN (ENGLISH)											
Swan		350									
SOWERBY WIDE PANEL (SOWERBY)											
Bowl	45										75 BA
SPANISH GALLEON (FENTON #570-5)											
Fan Vase	95										
SPANISH MOSS											
Hatpin Holder, 5½", rare	165										
Hatpin Holder, 8½", rare	235										
SPEARHEAD AND RIB (FENTON'S #916)											
Vase, 8" – 15"	70	135	140	95							

Pattern Name	M	A	G	B	PO	AO	IB	IG	W	Red	Other
SPEARHEAD AND RIB VARIANT (FENTON)											
Vase				175							
SPECTOR'S DEPARTMENT STORE											
See Heart and Vine (Fenton)											
SPHINX											
Paperweight, rare											600 AM
SPICE GRATER (INDIA)											
Pitcher	225										
Tumbler	90										
SPICE GRATER VARIANT (INDIA)											
Pitcher	225										
Tumbler	100										
SPICER BEEHIVE (SPICER STUDIOS)											
Honey Pot w/catch plate		95									110 AM
SPIDER WEB (NORTHWOOD)											
Candy Dish, covered											40 SM
SPIDER WEB (NORTHWOOD-DUGAN)											
Vase, two shapes	55		75								80 SM
SPIDER WEB AND TREEBARK (DUGAN)											
Vase, 6"	65										
SPIKED GRAPE AND VINE (JAIN)											
Tumbler	85										
SPIRAL (IMPERIAL)											
Candlesticks, pair	165	185	195								175 SM
SPIRALED DIAMOND POINT											
Vase, 6"	140										
SPIRALEX (DUGAN)											
Vase, 8" – 13"	35	75		150	75				85		
SPIRALS AND SPINES (NORTHWOOD)											
Vase, very rare									3000		
SPLIT DIAMOND (ENGLISH)											
Bowl, 8", scarce	40										
Bowl, 5", scarce	25										
Butter, very scarce	85										
Compote	55										
Creamer, small	25										
Sugar, open, scarce	30										
SPRING BASKET (IMPERIAL)											
Basket, handled, 5"	50										
SPRINGTIME (NORTHWOOD)											
Bowl, 5"	40	60	80								
Bowl, 9"	80	200	250								
Butter	250	400	475								
Creamer or Spooner	375	350	400								
Sugar	300	400	425								
Pitcher, rare	600	700	1100								
Tumbler, rare	130	145	120								
SPRY MEASURING CUP											
Measuring Cup	125										
SPUN FLOWERS											
Plate, 10", very scarce									75		
SPUN THREADS											
Hat Whimsey	55										
SQUARE DAISY AND BUTTON (IMPERIAL)											
Toothpick Holder, rare											125 SM
SQUARE DIAMOND											
Vase, rare	900			750							
S-REPEAT (DUGAN)											
Creamer, small		75									
Creamer Whimsey (from punch cup)		100									
Punch Bowl w/base, rare		4800									
Punch Cup, rare		100									
Sugar, rare (very light iridescence)		250									
Toothpick Holder (old only, rare)		90									
Tumbler	475	125									
SSSS'S											
Vase				125							
STAG AND HOLLY (FENTON)											
Bowl, ball footed, 9" – 13"	185	350	1000	400							1750 SA
Bowl, spatula footed, 8" – 10"	100	175	225	165						1600	275 AQ
Rose Bowl, footed, scarce	225		4600	3400							
Plate, 9", scarce	750	2500		3100							
Plate, 13", scarce	1000										
STAINED RIM (CZECH)											
Berry Bowl, footed, small	20										
Berry Bowl, footed, large	70										
STANDARD											
Vase, 5½"	50										
STAR											
Buttermilk Goblet	25										
Variant w/draped interior	30										

Pattern Name	M	A	G	B	PO	AO	IB	IG	W	Red	Other
STAR (ENGLISH)											
Bowl, 8"	50										
STAR AND DRAPE (CRYSTAL)											
Pitcher	165										
STAR AND FAN CORDIAL SET											
Cordial Set (decanter, four stemmed cordials, and tray)	625										900 AQ
STAR AND FILE (IMPERIAL)											
Bonbon	35										
Bowl, 7" – 9½"	30										40 CM
Bowl, handled	35										
Bowl, square	45										
Celery Vase, handled	50										50 CM
Champagne	35										
Compote	40										35 CM
Cordial	30										
Creamer or Sugar	30										45 CM
Custard Cup	30										
Decanter w/stopper	100										
Goblet	30										
Ice Tea Tumbler	70										
Juice Tumbler	50										
Juice Glass, stemmed, rare	650										
Lemonade Tumbler, rare	800										
Nut Bowl	45										70 CM
Pickle Dish	40										
Plate, 6"	60										
Pitcher	300										
Tumbler, rare	200										300 SM
Rose Bowl	75	175	125								150 AM
Sherbet	30										
Spooner	30										
Stemmed Ice Cream	60										50 CM
Wine	65								250		
STAR AND HOBS (NORTHERN LIGHTS)											
Rose Bowl, 7", rare	300			375							
Rose Bowl, 9", rare	250			350							
STARBURST (FINLAND)											
Creamer	35			55							
Rose Bowl	75			90							
Spittoon	600			900							2000 AM
Tumbler	150			325							
Vases, various shapes and sizes	375			600							500 AM
STARBURST AND DIAMONDS (FINLAND)											
Vase, 10½", scarce	350										
STARBURST AND FILE (SOWERBY)											
Sauce, four handles	95										
STARBURST LUSTRE (NORTHWOOD)											
Bowl	45	50	60								
Compote	55	65	80								
STARBURST PERFUME											
Perfume w/stopper	150										
STAR CENTER											
Bowl, 8½"	30	40									30 CM
Plate, 9"	60	80									80 CM
STAR CUT											
Decanter	100										
Tumbler	25										
STARDUST (FINLAND)											
Vase, 7¾"	85			145							
STARFISH (DUGAN)											
Bonbon, handled, scarce		200			165				325		
Compote	45	185	75		125						
STARFLOWER											
Pitcher, rare	6000			3500					18000		
STARFLOWER AND RIBS (INDIA)											
Pitcher	375										
Tumbler	95										
STARFLOWER AND ROLLS (INDIA)											
Pitcher	375										
Tumbler	95										
STARLYTE (IMPERIAL)											
Shade	100										
STAR GOBLET											
Goblet	25										
STAR MEDALLION (IMPERIAL)											
Bowl, 5" – 5½", dome footed	25								50		30 CM
Bowl, 7" – 9"	30										40 SM
Bowl, square, 7"	40										45 SM
Butter	100										
Celery Tray	60										50 CM
Compote	45										
Creamer, Spooner, Sugar, each	60										
Custard Cup	20										
Goblet	45										60 SM

Pattern Name	M	A	G	B	PO	AO	IB	IG	W	Red	Other
Handled Celery	80										65 SM
Ice Cream, stemmed, small	35										
Milk Pitcher	80		95								80 SM
Tumbler, two sizes	30		50								50 CM
Pickle Dish	40										
Plate, 5"	50										35 CM
Plate, 10"	70										85 CM
Vase, 6"	40										45 CM
STAR MEDALLION AND FAN											
Bowl, 7" – 9", scarce	65										
STAR MEDALLION W/FAN											
Bowl, 7" – 9", scarce	65										
STAR OF DAVID (IMPERIAL)											
Bowl, 8¾"	225	250	200							3000	100 SM
Bowl, round, 7½", rare	300										
STAR OF DAVID AND BOWS (NORTHWOOD)											
Bowl, 8½"	45	75	100								200 AM
STAR PAPERWEIGHT											
Paperweight, rare	1500										295 AM
STARRED SCROLL											
Hair Receiver	225										
STAR ROSETTE											
Decanter, very scarce	350										
Tumbler, very scarce	150										
STARS AND BARS											
Rose Bowl	130										
STARS AND BARS (CAMBRIDGE)											
Wine, rare	150										
STARS AND STRIPES (OLD GLORY)											
Plate, 7½", rare	150										
STARS OVER INDIA (JAIN)											
Tumbler	200										
STAR SPRAY (IMPERIAL)											
Bowl, 7"	35										40 SM
Bride's Basket, complete, rare	90										125 SM
Plate, 7½", scarce	75										95 SM
STATES, THE (U.S. GLASS)											
Bowl, 8", rare	175										
Butter, very rare	600										
Nappy, three handled, very rare			1200								
Shaker, very rare	500										
STERLING FURNITURE (FENTON)											
Bowl, advertising, rare		1000									
Plate, advertising, rare		1475									
Plate, advertising, handgrip		1800									
STIPPLED ACORNS (JEANNETTE)											
Covered Candy, footed	25	35		55							
STIPPLED BANDS AND PANELS											
Mug, very scarce	75										
STIPPLED CHERRY											
Tumbler	100										
STIPPLED DIAMONDS (MILLERSBURG)											
Card Tray Whimsey, two handled, very rare		2400									
Nappy, handled, very rare		2200	2300								2600 V
STIPPLED DIAMOND SWAG (ENGLISH)											
Compote	45		65	60							
STIPPLED ESTATE (ALBANY)											
Vase, 2½" – 5½"			60 – 90	70 – 100							95 – 120 AM
STIPPLED ESTATE (DUGAN)											
Bud Vase	150				200			225			
STIPPLED ESTATE (WESTMORELAND)											
Vase, 3"	125				150						
STIPPLED FLOWER (DUGAN)											
Bowl, 8½" (Add 25% for Lily of the Valley decoration)				85							
STIPPLED MUM (NORTHWOOD)											
Bowl, 9", scarce	65	90	100	200							
STIPPLED PETALS (DUGAN)											
Bowl, 9"		60		80							
Bowl, enameled decoration				175							
Handled Basket		150		170							
STIPPLED RAMBLER ROSE (DUGAN)											
Nut Bowl, footed	75			90							
STIPPLED RAYS (FENTON)											
Bonbon	30	40	50	45						350	
Bowl, 5" – 10"	35	45	55	50						350	115 AM
Bowl, square, ruffled, 8"	50	55	60								
Compote	30	40	45	40							300 CeB
Creamer or Sugar, each	25	75	75	55					75	450	
Plate, 7"	55	125	125	100						600	
Rose Bowl, very scarce	75	160	110								

84

Pattern Name	M	A	G	B	PO	AO	IB	IG	W	Red	Other
STIPPLED RAYS (NORTHWOOD)											
Bonbon	35	40	45	90							
Bowl, 8" – 10"	40	55	60	170							
Bowl, 11", very scarce		100							125		225 AQ
Compote	50	60	65								
Rose Bowl, very rare		950									
STIPPLED RAYS BREAKFAST SET											
Creamer, stemmed	30	85	70	50						300	85 SM
Sugar, stemmed	30	85	70	50						300	85 SM
Whimsey Sugar, rare	75	150	130	110						600	225 V
STIPPLED SALT CUP											
One Size	45										
STIPPLED STRAWBERRY (U.S. GLASS)											
Pitcher, rare	350										
Sherbet, stemmed	60										
Tumbler	95										
STJARNA (SWEDEN)											
Candy w/lid	225										
STORK (JENKINS)											
Vase	60								90		
STORK ABC											
Child's Plate, 7½"	75										
STORK AND RUSHES DUGAN)											
Basket, handled	125										
Bowl, 5"	30	30									
Bowl, 10"	40	50									
Butter, rare	150	175									
Creamer or Spooner, rare	80	90									
Hat	25	75		30							
Mug	25	175		1000							650 AQ
Punch Bowl w/base, rare	200	300		350							
Punch Cup	20	30		35							
Pitcher	250	225		500							
Tumbler	30	60		75							
Sugar, rare	90	120									
STOUGH'S THREE DOT											
Ray Gun Candy Container, rare	225										
STRAWBERRY (DUGAN)											
Epergne, rare		900									
STRAWBERRY (FENTON)											
Bonbon	50	75	90	140						450	375 LO
STRAWBERRY (NORTHWOOD)											
Bowl, 8" – 10" (stippled add 25%)	145	150	200	325	2750	25000		2000			450 G
Plate, handgrip, 7"	175	265	300								
Plate, 9"	250	325	285		4250						500 LV
Plate, stippled, 9"	2100	1050	1100	5000			23000	15500			
STRAWBERRY INTAGLIO (NORTHWOOD)											
Bowl, 5½"	30										
Bowl, 9½"	65										
STRAWBERRY POINT											
Tumbler	150										
STRAWBERRY SCROLL (FENTON)											
Pitcher, rare	3500			3000							
Tumbler, rare	160			135							
STRAWBERRY SPRAY											
Brooch				175							
STRAWBERRY W/ CHECKERBOARD (JENKINS)											
Butter	85										
Creamer or Sugar	35										
Spooner	45										
STRAWBERRY WREATH (MILLERSBURG)											
Banana Boat Whimsey, rare		2000	2000								2600 V
Bowl, 6½" – 7½"	75	150	200								1800 V
Bowl, 6½" – 7½", very scarce	150	200	250								
Bowl, 8" – 10", scarce	185	275	300								1500 V
Bowl, 9", square	325	400	425								
Bowl, tricornered, 9½"	450	650	750								
Compote, scarce	350	300	400								2100 V
Gravy Boat Whimsey, rare											3000 V
STREAMLINE (CRYSTAL)											
Creamer	60										
Sugar w/lid	80										
STREAM OF HEARTS (FENTON)											
Compote, rare	150										
Goblet, rare	225										
STRETCH											
Punch Bowl and Base										3500	
STRETCHED DIAMOND (NORTHWOOD)											
Tumbler, rare	175										
STRETCHED DIAMONDS AND DOTS											
Tumbler	175										
STRING OF BEADS											
One Shape	35		40								

Pattern Name	M	A	G	B	PO	AO	IB	IG	W	Red	Other
STRUTTING PEACOCK (WESTMORELAND)											
Creamer or Sugar w/lid		100	100								
Rose Bowl Whimsey			150								175 BA
STUDS (JEANNETTE)											
(Depression Era, Holiday, Buttons and Bows) (Many shapes and sizes, from $5 to $145)											
STYLE (CRYSTAL)											
Bowl, 8"	100	145									
STYLIZED FLOWER CENTER (FENTON)											
Center design on some Orange Tree bowls and plates											
SUMMER DAYS (DUGAN)											
Vase, 6"	50	90		125							
(Note: This is actually the base for the Stork and Rushes punch set.)											
SUNBEAM (MCKEE)											
Whiskey, scarce	125										
SUNFLOWER (MILLERSBURG)											
Pin Tray, scarce	800	600	625								
SUNFLOWER (NORTHWOOD)											
Bowl, 8½"	95	175	165	700		13000	1750				800 ReB
Plate, rare	600	1250									
SUNFLOWER AND DIAMOND											
Vase, two sizes	300			500							
SUNGOLD											
Epergne											450 AM
SUNGOLD FLORA (BROCKWITZ)											
Bowl, 9", rare	300										
SUNK DAISY *AKA AMERIKA											
Bowl	225	375		275							
Rose Bowl, three sizes, rare	350	150		500							
SUNK DIAMOND BAND (U.S. GLASS)											
Pitcher, rare	150								250		
Tumbler, rare	50								75		
SUNKEN DAISY (ENGLISH)											
Sugar	30			40							
SUNKEN HOLLYHOCK											
Lamp, Gone with the Wind, rare	4000								12000		
SUN PUNCH											
Bottle	30								35		
SUNRAY											
Compote		45			60						
SUNRAY (FENTON)											
Compote (iridized milk glass)											110 MO
SUPERB DRAPE (NORTHWOOD)											
Vase, very rare	1700		3000			5000					2000 V
SUPERSTAR (BROCKWITZ)											
Jardiniere				295							
SVEA (AKA: SWEDEN)											
Bowls, various	75 – 100			100 – 145							
Bonboniere w/lid, rare				250							
Plate, 6"				275							
Rose Bowl, small, 5½"	100			175							
Rose Bowl, large, 8"	175	325		300							
Trays, various	45 – 85			60 – 110							
Vase, 9", scarce	110			225							
Vase, 4", rare				350							
SVEA VARIANT											
Vase, various sizes, very scarce				200 – 375							
SWAN (AUSTRALIAN)											
Bowl, 5"	150	170									
Bowl, 9"	225	400									
SWANS AND FLOWERS (JAIN)											
Tumbler, rare	300										
SWEETHEART (CAMBRIDGE)											
Cookie Jar w/lid, rare	1550		1100								
Tumbler, rare	650										
SWIRL (IMPERIAL)											
Bowl	40										
Candlestick, each	35										
Mug, rare	90										
Plate	80										
Vase	40										
SWIRL AND VARIANTS (NORTHWOOD)											
Pitcher	225		700								
Tumbler	75		125								
Whimsey Pitcher, no handle	300										
SWIRLED GUM TIP VARIANT											
Vase											500 BA
SWIRLED MORNING GLORY (IMPERIAL)											
Vase	40	75									90 SM
SWIRLED RIB (NORTHWOOD)											
Pitcher	165										

Pattern Name	M	A	G	B	PO	AO	IB	IG	W	Red	Other
Tumbler	70	75									
SWIRLED THREADS											
Goblet	95										
SWIRLED THREADS AND OPTIC											
Vase, 6"	80										
SWIRL HOBNAIL (MILLERSBURG)											
Rose Bowl, scarce	300	1000									
Spittoon, scarce	500	750	4000								
Vase, 7" – 14", scarce	250	275	700	5800							
SWIRL PANEL SHAKER											
Shaker, each	45										
SWIRL VARIANT (IMPERIAL)											
Bowl, 7" – 8"	30										
Cake Plate											85 CL
Dessert, stemmed	30										
Epergne			200		50						
Juice Glass	40										
Pitcher, 7½"	100										
Plate, 6" – 8¼"	50		60		65						75 CL
Vase, 6½"	35		45		200				70		
SWORD AND CIRCLE											
Tumbler, rare	150									600	
Juice Tumbler, rare	225										
SYDNEY (FOSTORIA)											
Tumbler, rare	700										
SYRUP SET											
Two Piece Set	135										
TAFFETA LUSTRE (FOSTORIA)											
Candlesticks, pair, very scarce		300	350	400							450 AM
Compote, rare											325 BA
Console Bowl, 11", rare		150	150	175							200 AM
(Add 25% for old paper labels attached)											
Perfume w/stopper	100	150									175 LV
TALL HAT											
Various sizes, 4" – 10"	40										50 PK
TALL 24 CRUET											
Cruet, 6½"	100										
TARENTUM'S VIRGINIA											
Spooner, rare	250										
TARGET (DUGAN)											
Vase, 5" – 7"	40	250		225	140				150		225 LV
Vase, 8" – 13"	25	175	425	175	65						400 V
TASSELS											
Shade											100 IM
TCHECO (CZECH)											
Vase, 9"		65									
TEN MUMS (FENTON)											
Bowl, footed, 9", scarce	450	650									
Bowl, flat, 8" – 10"	300	275	300	375							
Plate, 10", rare				1900							
Pitcher, rare	500			800					3000		
Tumbler, rare	75			100					300		
TENNESSEE STAR (RIIHIMAKI)											
Vase	425			500							600 AM
Vase Whimsey, small				700							
TEN PANEL BREAKFAST SET											
Creamer		90									
Sugar		80									
TEN POINTED STAR (HIGBEE)											
Mug	250										
TEXAS (U.S. GLASS)											
Breakfast Creamer or Sugar, each											75 LV
TEXAS TUMBLER (BROCKWITZ)											
Giant Tumbler (vase)	625			500							
TEXAS HEADDRESS (WESTMORELAND)											
Punch Cup	45										
THIN AND WIDE RIB (NORTHWOOD)											
Vase, ruffled	35	60	60	125			275	300			600 IL
Vase, J.I.P. shape	85	175	175	240							250 TL
THIN RIB (FENTON)											
Candlesticks, pair	80									450	
Vase, 7" – 17"	35	60	60	70						2800	150 AM
THIN RIB (NORTHWOOD)											
Exterior pattern only											
THIN RIB AND DRAPE											
Vase, 4" – 11"	125	225	200	900							
THIN RIB SHADE (NORTHWOOD)											
Shade	75										
THISTLE (ENGLISH)											
Vase, 6"	105										
THISTLE (FENTON)											
Bowl, 8" – 10"	45	65	80	95							290 AQ
Bowl, advertising (Horlacher)		250	225								
Plate, 9", very scarce	6700	4100	3750								
THISTLE											
Shade	60										

Pattern Name	M	A	G	B	PO	AO	IB	IG	W	Red	Other
THISTLE AND LOTUS (FENTON)											
Bowl, 7"	55		75	70							
THISTLE AND THORN (ENGLISH)											
Bowl, footed, 6"	50										
Creamer or Sugar, each	60										
Nut Bowl	75										
Plate/low Bowl, footed, 8½"	100										
THISTLE BANANA BOAT (FENTON)											
Banana Boat, footed, scarce	150	325	450	300							
THREAD AND CANE (CRYSTAL)											
Compote	90	150									
Salver	110	175									
THREADED BUTTERFLIES (U.S. GLASS)											
Plate, footed, very rare											6500 AQ
THREADED PETALS (SOWERBY)											
Bowl, 6", rare	200										
THREADED SIX PANEL											
Bud Vase, 7¾"	75										
THREADED WIDE PANEL											
Candy w/lid, two sizes	75							125		275	
Goblet	50			125				85		165	
THREADED WIDE PANEL VARIANT											
Goblet				100							
THREADS (CRYSTAL)											
Compote	75	145									
THREE DIAMONDS											
Tumble-up, three pieces	175										
Vase, 6" – 10"	45	50	60	75	75						60 CM
THREE FACE											
Compote w/lid, 6",	325										
THREE FLOWERS (IMPERIAL)											
Tray, center handle, 12"	60										70SM
THREE FOOTER (EDA)											
Bowl, footed, 8"	175			300							450 LV
THREE FRUITS (NORTHWOOD)											
Bowl, 9"	100	225	300			1700	1150	1350			1000 LGO
Bowl, 9", stippled	225	325	650	500		1550	3900	2600			3000 SA
Bowl, 8", stippled, proof, very rare											700 IC
Plate, 9"	300	400	400	850		2900	9000	11500			450 LV
Plate, 9", stippled	400	650	2500	800		7000	6000	8500			8000 HO
THREE FRUITS BANDED											
*Photo for illustration only. Prices same as regular Three Fruits pattern.											
THREE FRUITS INTAGLIO (NORTHWOOD)											
Bowl, footed, 6", very rare	750										
THREE FRUITS MEDALLION (NORTHWOOD)											
Bowl, spatula footed or dome base, 8" – 9½" (*Stippled add 25%)	100	150	185	500		1300	900	375	475		550 IC
THREE FRUITS VARIANT											
Bowl, 8" – 9"	100	200	250								
Plate, 12 sided	135	200	200	225							
THREE-IN-ONE (IMPERIAL)											
Banana Bowl Whimsey, scarce	100										
Bowl, 4½"	20	40	30								30 SM
Bowl, 8¾"	30	60	40								75 AM
Plate, 6½"	75										95 SM
Rose Bowl, rare	125										
Toothpick Holder, rare (variant)	75										
Tricornered Whimsey, rare	250										
THREE MONKEYS											
Bottle, rare											90 CL
THREE RING MINI SHOT											
Miniature Shot Glass	75										
THREE RIVERS VARIANT											
Pickle Castor (*age?)	225										
THREE ROLL											
Tumble-Up, complete	90										
THREE ROW (IMPERIAL)											
Vase, rare	2400	2900									4500 SM
THUMBPRINT AND OVAL (IMPERIAL)											
Vase, 5½", rare	400	1700									
THUMBPRINT AND SPEARS											
Creamer	50		60								
TIERED PANELS											
Cup, scarce	30										
TIERED THUMBPRINT											
Bowls, two sizes	45										
Candlesticks, pair	120										
TIERS											
Bowl, 9"	40										
Tumbler	60										
TIGER LILY (FINLAND)											
Pitcher, rare				950							
Tumbler, rare				450							

Pattern Name	M	A	G	B	PO	AO	IB	IG	W	Red	Other
TIGER LILY (IMPERIAL)											
Hat Whimsey from Tumbler			200								
Pitcher	140	550	300								400 TL
Tumbler	25	145	50	225							100 OG
TINY BERRY											
Tumbler, 2¼"				45							
TINY BUBBLES											
Vase, 8½"			225								
TINY BLUB VASE											
Miniature Vase, 2"	50										
TINY DAISY (SOWERBY)											
Butter	245										
Creamer											125 V
TINY HAT											
Hat Shape, 1¾"				75							
TINY HOBNAIL											
Lamp	110										
TINY RIB											
Vase, 8" – 10"	75										
TINY THUMBPRINT											
Creamer, lettered	25										
TOKIO (EDA)											
Bowl				225							
Vase, 7½"				350							
TOLTEC (MCKEE)											
Butter (ruby iridized), rare		375									
Pitcher, tankard, very rare	2600										
TOMAHAWK (CAMBRIDGE)											
One Size, rare				3000							
TOMATO BAND (CZECH)											
Liquor Set, complete	175										
TOP HAT											
Vase, 9½"	35								50		
TORCHIERE											
Candlesticks, pair	75										
TORNADO (NORTHWOOD)											
Vase, plain, two sizes	400	425	550	1200					1000		550 HO
Vase, ribbed, 2 sizes	450	500		2000			7250		1250		
Vase Whimsey, very scarce											2200 WS
Vase Whimsey Rose Bowl, very rare		3500									
Vase Whimsey, tricorner top, very rare											4500 SA
Vase, ruffled, very rare		1400									
TORNADO VARIANT (NORTHWOOD)											
Vase, rare	1700										
TOWERS (ENGLISH)											
Hat Vase	65										
TOWN PUMP (NORTHWOOD)											
One Shape, rare	2250	900	3500								
TOY PUNCH SET (CAMBRIDGE)											
Bowl only, footed	100										
TRACERY (MILLERSBURG)											
Bonbon, rare		1300	1100								
TRAILING FLOWERS (CRYSTAL)											
Bowl, 7"	175										
TREE BARK (IMPERIAL)											
Bowl, 7½"	15										
Candlesticks, 4½", pair	40										
Candlesticks, 7", pair	55										
Candy Jar w/lid	35										
Console Bowl	35										
Pickle Jar, 7½"	55										
Pitcher, open top	50										100 AM
Pitcher w/lid	75										
Plate, 8"	50										
Sauce Bowl, 4"	15										
Tumbler, two sizes	25										
Vase	30										
TREE BARK VARIANT											
Candleholder on Stand	75										
Juice	20										
Planter	60										
Pitcher	60										
Tumbler	20										
Vase	30										
TREE OF LIFE											
Bowl, 5½"	25										
Basket, handled	25										
Perfumer w/lid	35										
Plate, 7½"	35										
Pitcher	60										
Tumbler	30										
Tumbler, juice, rare	75										
Rose Bowl, two sizes	40										
Vase Whimsey, from pitcher											150 CL
TREE OF LIFE (DUGAN)											
Vase, rare			150	175							
TREE OF LIFE BASE (NORTHWOOD)											
Compote, 6", rare											550 IC

Pattern Name	M	A	G	B	PO	AO	IB	IG	W	Red	Other
TREE TRUNK (NORTHWOOD)											
Jardiniere Whimsey, rare		4000									
Vase, squat, 5" – 8"	60	165	200	800			1000	600			
Vase, standard, 8" – 12"	75	100	125	250		1200	550	400	200		400 SA
Vase, mid size, 12" – 15"	325	375	325	700		3000	1600	1400	1300		3600 LG
Vase, funeral, 12" – 22"	4000	5000	5500	5000			26000	28500	3000		
Vase, J.I.P., very rare	3500	9500									
(Add 300% for Elephant Foot or Plunger base)											
TREFOIL FINE CUT (MILLERSBURG)											
Plate, 11½", very rare	14000										
TREVOR'S TESSELATED ROSE											
Light Fixture	225										
TRIANDS (ENGLISH)											
Butter	65										
Celery Vase	55										
Compote, small scarce	75										
Creamer, Sugar, or Spooner	50										
TRIBAL (INDIA)											
Vase	175										
TRINKET BOX											
Lidded Box, with or without lettering	100										
TRIPLE ALLIANCE (BROCKWITZ)											
Biscuit Jar	200			350							
TRIPLE BAND AND PANELS											
Decanter w/stopper	125										
TRIPLETS (DUGAN)											
Bowl, 6" – 8"	25	30	65		75						125 V
Hat	30	40	70								
TROPICANA											
Vase, rare	1600										
TROUT AND FLY (MILLERSBURG)											
Bowl, 8¾" (various shapes)	400	550	700								700 LV
Plate, 9", rare	8500	10000	14000								25000 LV
TRUMPET (DUGAN)											
Candlesticks, each								65			
TSUNAMI (EUROPEAN)											
Bowl, 10"	110										
TULIP (MILLERSBURG)											
Compote, 9", rare	1600	1500	1800								
TULIP AND CANE (IMPERIAL)											
Bowl	35										
Claret Goblet, rare	175										
Goblet, 8 oz., rare	100										
Jelly Compote, ruffled, 5", rare	150										
Nappy, handled, very rare	200										
Wine, two sizes, rare	85										
TULIP AND CORD (FINLAND)											
Mug, handled	125										
TULIP PANELS											
Ginger Jar	125										
TULIP SCROLL (MILLERSBURG)											
Vase, 6" – 12", rare	550	750	850								
TUMBLE-UP (FENTON-IMPERIAL)											
Plain, complete	85						375				
Handled, complete, rare	295										320 V
TUSCAN COLUMN											
Vase Whimsey, 3"			125								
TWELVE RINGS											
Candlesticks, each	45										
TWIGS (DUGAN)											
Tall Vase	30	70									
Squat Vase, very scarce	300	1100				2300					
TWIG WITH FANS											
Shaker		125									
TWIN GOLDEN THISTLE											
Tray, 10½" x 6"	275										
TWINS (IMPERIAL)											
Bowl, 5"	15		30								20 CM
Bowl, 9"	35		50								40 CM
Fruit Bowl w/base	80										
TWIST											
Candlesticks, pair	125										
TWISTED OPTIC (IMPERIAL)											
(Depression era, many shapes and sizes, from $5 to $75)											
TWISTED RIB (DUGAN)											
Vase, various sizes	35	75		150	75				85		
TWISTER (JAIN)											
Tumbler	175										
TWITCH (BARTLETT-COLLINS)											
Creamer	30										
Cup	30										
Sherbet	45										
TWO FLOWERS (FENTON)											
Bowl, footed, 6" – 7"	25	60	65	55							
Bowl, footed, 8" – 10"	75	325	250	225						5500	1650 SM

Pattern Name	M	A	G	B	PO	AO	IB	IG	W	Red	Other
Bowl, spatula footed, 8"	90	110	140	110							
Bowl, 8" – 9", flat, rare	150									1800	135 V
Plate, footed, 9"	700		675	650							
Plate, 13", rare	2200										
Rose Bowl, rare	125	150	450	175						7000	
Rose Bowl, giant, rare	250			800					375	4500	500 SM
TWO FORTY NINE											
Candleholders, pair									700		
TWO FRUITS (FENTON)											
Bonbon, flat, either shape, scarce	65	125	200	100					140		300 V
TWO HANDLED SWIRL (IMPERIAL)											
Vase	50										75 SM
TWO ROW (IMPERIAL)											
Vase, rare		1150									
UNIVERSAL HOME BOTTLE											
One Shape	125										
UNPINCHED RIB											
Vase	85										225 AM
UNSHOD											
Pitcher	85										
URN											
Vase, 9"	25										
US DIAMOND BLOCK (U.S. GLASS)											
Compote, rare	65				90						
Shakers, pair, scarce	80										
U.S. #310 (U.S. GLASS)											
Bowl, 10"								75			
Candy w/lid								90			
Cheese Set								90			
Compote								65			
Mayonnaise Set								95			
Plate								60			
Vase								85			
U.S. GLASS #15021											
Vase, 22"	125										
U.S. GLASS SLIPPER											
Novelty Slipper	75										
U.S. REGAL											
Bowl, very scarce	150										
Cup, stemmed, with handle	100										
Sherbet, stemmed, with handle	125										
UTAH LIQUOR (FENTON)											
Bowl, advertising, scarce		850									
Plate, advertising, scarce		1350									
Plate, advertising, handgrip, scarce		1600									
UTILITY											
Lamp, 8", complete	90										
VALENTINE											
Ring Tray	80										
VALENTINE (NORTHWOOD)											
Bowl, 5", scarce	100	225									
Bowl, 10", scarce	400										
VENETIAN											
Bowl, 10½", rare	500										
Butter, rare	950										
Creamer, rare	500										
Sugar, rare	625										
Vase (lamp base), 9¼", rare	1000		1400								
VERA											
Vase	125	325		325							
VICTORIAN (DUGAN)											
Bowl, 10" – 12", rare		350			2500						
Bowl, ice cream shape, rare		1000									
VICTORIAN HAND VASE											
Fancy Vase											275 LV
VICTORIAN TRUMPET VASE											
Vase, various painted designs, rare	700										
VINELAND (DUGAN)											
Candlesticks, each							70				
VINEYARD (DUGAN)											
Pitcher	120	350		1300							
Tumbler	20	50							250		
VINEYARD AND FISHNET											
Vase, rare										675	
VINEYARD HARVEST (JAIN)											
Tumbler, rare	250										
VINING DAISIES (ARGENTINA)											
Decanter	150										
VINING LEAF AND VARIANTS (ENGLISH)											
Rose Bowl, rare	250										
Spittoon, rare	350										
Vase, rare	225		350								
VINING TWIGS (DUGAN)											
Bowl, 7½"	35	45	50								
Hat	40	50							65		

Pattern Name	M	A	G	B	PO	AO	IB	IG	W	Red	Other
Plate, 7", rare									425		300 LV
VINLOV (SWEDEN)											
Banana Boat	175	325									
VINTAGE (DUGAN)											
Dresser Tray, 7" x 11"	85										
Perfume w/stopper	395	600									
Powder Jar w/lid	70	225		300					300		
VINTAGE (FENTON)											
Bonbon	35	50	70	60							55 PB
Bowl, 4½"	20	35	40	40							
Bowl, 6", tricorner	30	60	80	70							
Bowl, 6½" – 7"	30	40	45	45		475				3900	100 V
Bowl, 8" – 9"	40	45	50	50		3700				2000	750 PeB
Bowl, 10"	45	60	90	110						5000	130 V
Compote	40	50	55	60							
Epergne, one lily, two sizes	125	165	145	145							
Fernery, two variations	55	100	135	115						550	625 AM
Plate, 6" – 8"	200	300	325	275							
Plate, 9", very scarce	3900	4000	4000								
Punch Bowl w/base (Wreath of Roses exterior)	300	450	500	450							
Punch Cup	25	35	40	35							
Rose Bowl	95			125							
Spittoon Whimsey	6500										
Vase Whimsey, from epergne											
Base, very rare	1500										
Whimsey Fernery		425									
Whimsey, from punch bowl, very rare		1500									
VINTAGE (MILLERSBURG)											
Bowl, 5", rare	800		1100	2500							
Bowl, 9", rare	700	950	825	400							
VINTAGE (NORTHWOOD)											
Bowl, 8" – 9"	60	75	90								100 BA
VINTAGE (U.S. GLASS)											
Wine	40	50									
VINTAGE BANDED (DUGAN)											
Mug	20	600									500 SM
Pitcher	325	800									
Tumbler, rare	300										
VINTAGE VARIANT (DUGAN)											
Bowl, footed 8½"	85	175	250	200							900 CeB
Plate	300	575									
VIOLET BASKETS											
Basket, either type	40	50		95							
VIRGINIA (BANDED PORTLAND)											
See Banded Portland (U.S. Glass)											
VIRGINIA BLACKBERRY (U.S. GLASS)											
Pitcher, small, rare				950							
(Note: Tiny Berry mini tumbler may match this)											
VOGUE (FOSTORIA)											
Toothpick Holder, scarce	250										
VOLTEC (MCKEE)											
Covered Butter		150									
VOTIVE LIGHT (MEXICAN)											
Candle Vase, 4½", rare	450										
WAFFLE											
Open Sugar or Creamer	65										
WAFFLE BLOCK (IMPERIAL)											
Basket, handled, 10"	50										175 TL
Bowl, 7" – 9"	30										
Bowl, 8" square	45										
Bowl, 11½"	55										65 CM
Butter	100										
Creamer	60										
Nappy	40										65 CM
Parfait Glass, stemmed	30										35 CM
Pitcher	125										150 CM
Punch Bowl and Base	110										165 CM
Tumbler, scarce	275										350 CM
Tumbler Variant, rare											500 CM
Plate, 6"	30										40 CM
Plate, 10" – 12", any shape	90										150 CM
Punch Bowl	175										250 TL
Punch Cup	20										35 TL
Rose Bowl	75										
Shakers, pair	75										
Sherbet											35 CM
Spittoon, scarce	75										85 CM
Sugar	60										
Vase, 8" – 11"	40										55 CM
WAFFLE BLOCK AND HOBSTAR (IMPERIAL)											
Basket, handled	250										265 SM
WAFFLE WEAVE											
Inkwell	95										

Pattern Name	M	A	G	B	PO	AO	IB	IG	W	Red	Other
WAGNER (WESTMORELAND)											
Bowl, low round	25										
WAGON WHEEL											
Candy w/lid, enameled	45										
WAR DANCE (ENGLISH)											
Compote, 5"	120										
WASHBOARD											
Butter	70										
Creamer, 5½"	45										
Punch Cup	15										
Tumbler	85										
WATER LILY (FENTON)											
Bonbon	40										
Bowl, footed, 5"	50		200	115						1100	155 V
Bowl, footed, 10"	90	140	400	225						3500	200 BA
Chop Plate, 11", very rare	4500										
*(Add 10% for variant with lily center)											
WATER LILY AND CATTAILS (FENTON)											
Bonbon	60	85		90							
Berry Bowl, small	35	50		50							
Berry Bowl, large	50			180							
Bowl, 6", tricorner	35										
Bowl, 10½", very rare			600								
Butter	175										
Creamer or Spooner	75										
Sugar	100										
Pitcher	340			5500							
Tumbler	60										
Spittoon Whimsey, rare	2500										
Vase Whimsey or Jardiniere	275										
WATER LILY AND CATTAILS (NORTHWOOD)											
Pitcher	400			6000							
Tumbler	75	250		700							
Tumbler (etched name)				1700							
WATER LILY AND DRAGONFLY (AUSTRALIAN)											
Float Bowl, 10½", complete	150	185									
WEBBED CLEMATIS											
Lamp, rare											1500 BA
Vase, 12½"	250										
WEEPING CHERRY (DUGAN)											
Bowl, footed	90	130		275							
Bowl, flat	75	110									
WESTERN DAISY											
Bowl, rare			450		325						
WESTERN THISTLE											
Cider Pitcher				350							
Tumbler, rare	340			250							
Tumbler Whimsey, rare	300										225 AM
Vase, rare	325										
WESTERN THISTLE VARIANT											
Berry Bowl, small	35										
Berry Bowl, large	70										
Compote, small	100										
Vase	250										
WESTMORELAND #750 BASKET											
Basket, small	25										
Basket, large	45										
WESTMORELAND #1700											
Sugar, open, handled											75 AM
Lilly Vase, 6" – 9"		125 – 175									
WESTMORELAND #1776											
Compote, tall stemmed		95									
WESTMORELAND COLONIAL LILY VASE											
Vase, 6" (age questionable)		125									325 V
WHEAT (NORTHWOOD)											
Bowl, w/lid, very rare		8000									
Sherbet, very rare		6000									
Sweetmeat w/lid, very rare		8000	9500								
WHEAT SHEAF (CAMBRIDGE)											
Decanter, very rare		4000									
WHEELS (IMPERIAL)											
Bowl, 8" – 9"	50										
Bowl, 5½"	20										30 CM
WHIRLING HOBSTAR											
Cup	40										
Pitcher	200										
Child's Punch Bowl and Base	125										
WHIRLING LEAVES (MILLERSBURG)											
Bowl, 9" – 11", round ruffled or three in one edge	135	250	250	4750							2600 V
Bowl, square, very scarce	400	500	600								
Bowl, 10", tricornered	385	425	475								3500 V
WHIRLING STAR (IMPERIAL)											
Bowl, 9" – 11"	40										

Pattern Name	M	A	G	B	PO	AO	IB	IG	W	Red	Other
Compote	55		85								
Punch Bowl w/base	125										400 AQ
Punch Cup	10										25 AQ
WHIRLSAWAY (JAIN)											
Tumbler, two sizes, two shapes	275										
WHIRLWIND											
Bowl					125						
WHITE ELEPHANT											
Ornament, rare									350		
WHITE OAK											
Tumbler, rare	200										
WICKERWORK (ENGLISH)											
Bowl w/base, complete	250	400									
WIDE PANEL (FENTON)											
Covered Candy Dish	40	65							70		100 CeB
Lemonade Glass, handled	30										
Vase, 7" – 9"	30	40	50	60						400	
WIDE PANEL (IMPERIAL)											
Bowl, 7" – 10"	40	100								250	125 MMG
Bowl, square, 6", scarce	50										45 CM
Bowl, master, 11" – 12"	65										175 AM
Bowl, console, 13"+, rare										900	
Plate, 6"	25										25 CM
Plate, 8"	50									200	250 SM
Plate, 10" – 11"	75								75	400	75 CM
Rose Bowl, 6½" – 8"									75		
Rose Bowl, giant, scarce	150										175 SM
Underplate, 14" – 15"	85									750	150 SM
Spittoon Whimsey, large, rare	550										
Spittoon Whimsey, medium, rare	400										
Spittoon Whimsey, small, rare	250										
WIDE PANEL (MILLERSBURG)											
Bowl, 9", scarce	125										
Bowl, 4" – 5", very scarce	50										
*Also a secondary pattern on some bowls and plates.											
WIDE PANEL (NORTHWOOD)											
Bowl, 8" – 9", very scarce	50		75								
Compote (#645)	40										85 V
Console Set (bowl and two candlesticks)	75										175 V
Covered Candy Dish	45						100				
Epergne, four lily, scarce	900	1300	1250	1900		26000	13500	14000	2800		
Vase from epergne lily, rare			400								
WIDE PANEL (U.S. GLASS)											
Salt	50										
WIDE PANEL (WESTMORELAND)											
Bowl, 7½"											60 TL
Bowl, 8¼"											75 TL
WIDE PANEL AND DIAMOND											
Vase, 6¼"	150										200 BA
WIDE PANEL BOUQUET											
Basket, 3½"	75										
WIDE PANEL CHERRY											
Pitcher w/lid, rare	1200								195		
WIDE PANEL SHADE											
Lightshade	95		175								
WIDE PANEL VARIANT (NORTHWOOD)											
Pitcher, tankard	200	275	300								
WIDE PETALS											
Stemmed Salt Dip	100										
WIDE RIB (DUGAN)											
Vase, squat, 4" – 6"	30	100			65						
Vase, standard, 7" – 12"	25	75		150	50						165 AQ
Spittoon Whimsey from vase, 5½", rare					125						
WIDE RIB (NORTHWOOD)											
Jardiniere Whimsey, 4", rare		800	700								300 LG
Vase, squat, 5" – 7"	50	60	65	125					120		425 V
Vase, standard, 8" – 14"	40	50	50	110		1300					1000 SA
Vase, funeral, 15" – 22"	300	350	375	725							
(J.I.P. add 25%)											
WIDE SWIRL											
Milk Pitcher	100										
WIGWAM (HEISEY)											
Tumbler, rare	150										
WILD BERRY											
Powder Jar w/lid	450										
Powder Jar Variant w/lid											425 BO
WILD BLACKBERRY (FENTON)											
Bowl, 8½", scarce	100	150	175	300							
Bowl, advertising (Maday), rare		600	1100								
Plate, very rare		8500									
WILD FERN (AUSTRALIAN)											
Compote	200	275									
WILDFLOWER (MILLERSBURG)											
Compote, jelly, rare	1300	1700									

Pattern Name	M	A	G	B	PO	AO	IB	IG	W	Red	Other
Compote, ruffled, rare	900	1300	1800								
WILDFLOWER (NORTHWOOD)											
Compote (plain interior)	250	300	300	425							
WILD GRAPE											
Bowl, 8¾", very scarce	125										
WILD LOGANBERRY (PHOENIX)											
Cider Pitcher, rare											520 IM
Compote, covered, rare											295 IM
Creamer, rare											150 IM
Goblet					150						
Sugar, rare											100 IM
Wine	145										
(*Also known as Dewberry)											
WILD ROSE											
Bowl, 8½", rare	100										
Syrup, rare	600										
WILD ROSE (MILLERSBURG)											
Lamp, small, rare	1000	1200	1850								
Lamp, medium, rare	1200	1500	2200								
Medallion Lamp, rare	2400	2400	2400								
Lamp, marked Riverside, very rare			3000								
WILD ROSE (NORTHWOOD)											
Bowl, footed, open edge, 6"	75	120	100	300		8000					300 HO
WILD ROSE SHADE											
Lampshade	95										
WILD ROSE WREATH (MINIATURE INTAGLIO)											
Nut Cup, stemmed, rare	250					575 BO			700		600 AQ
WILD STRAWBERRY (NORTHWOOD)											
Bowl, 6", rare	75	150	250				225	275	125		
Bowl, 9" – 10½"	95	125	300				1100	1650	400		1650 LG
Plate, 7" – 9", handgrip, scarce	200	225	225								
WILLS'S GOLD FLAKE											
Ashtray	75										
WINDFLOWER (DUGAN)											
Bowl, 8½"	30	75		125							800 V
Nappy, handled	45	95		250	200			200			
Plate, 9"	125	300		325							
Plate, decorated, very rare	425										
WINDMILL (IMPERIAL)											
Bowl, 5"	20	25	25								125 VI
Bowl, 9"	35	175	40								200 V
Bowl, footed, 9"	30	70	55								90 SM
Fruit Bowl, 10½"	40		40								
Milk Pitcher	80	475	140								275 SM
Pitcher	170	350	175								200 PB
Tumbler	50	150	45								175 AM
Pickle Dish	30	200	85								75 CM
Tray, flat	30	250	85								75 CM
WINDMILL AND CHECKERBOARD											
Dutch Plate, 8", late	15										
WINDSOR FLOWER ARRANGER (CZECH)											
Flower Arranger, rare	100						125				95 PK
WINE AND ROSES (FENTON)											
Cider Pitcher, scarce	450										
Compote, ruffled, rare	150										
Wine Goblet	90			100		600					145 AQ
WINGED HEAVY SHELL											
Vase, 3½"									95		
WINKEN											
Lamp	125										
WINTER BOOT											
Miniature Boot Novelty	50										
WINTERLILY (DUGAN)											
Vase, footed, 5½", very rare	850										
WISE OWL											
Bank	30										
WISHBONE											
Flower Arranger	75										90 PK
WISHBONE (NORTHWOOD)											
Bowl, flat, 8" – 10"	150	500	900	1650			925		400		575 EmG
Bowl, footed, 7½" – 9"	150	175	250	1150		5000	1500	1500	400		475 HO
Epergne, rare	350	650	850				3800	5000	1700		3000 LG
Plate, footed, 9", rare	2000	400	1000								
Plate, flat, 10", rare	4000	2500	3500								
Pitcher, rare	800	1100	900								
Tumbler, scarce	100	125	125								2200 PL
WISHBONE AND SPADES (DUGAN)											
Bowl, 5"		225			190						
Bowl, 10"		400			325						
Bowl, tricorner or banana shape					375						
Plate, 6", rare		600		2000	300						
Plate, 10½", rare		2000			1800						
WISTERIA (NORTHWOOD)											
Bank Whimsey, rare									3500		
Pitcher, rare							13000		4700		
Tumbler, rare							600	525	450		

Pattern Name	M	A	G	B	PO	AO	IB	IG	W	Red	Other
Vase Whimsey, very rare			22000								
WITCHES POT											
One Shape, souvenir	300										
WOODEN SHOE											
One Shape, rare	175										
WOODLANDS VASE											
Vase, 5", rare	235										
WOODPECKER (DUGAN)											
Wall Vase	165										120 V
WOODPECKER AND IVY											
Vase, very rare	4500		6000								7500 V
WORLD BANK											
Bank, 4½"	100										
WREATHED BLEEDING HEARTS (DUGAN)											
Vase, 5¼"	125										
WREATHED CHERRY (DUGAN)											
Bowl, oval, 5"	25	40		125	100				60		65 BA
Bowl, oval, 10½" – 12"	90	140		300	400				175		150 BA
Butter	125	275							225		
Creamer or Spooner	65	80							80		
Pitcher	400	550							850		
Tumbler	90	100							100		
Sugar	70	110							110		
Toothpick, old only		175									
WREATHED MEDALLION											
Oil Lamp	150										
WREATH OF ROSES (DUGAN)											
Nut Bowl	70										
Rose Bowl Whimsey, scarce	125	150									
Tricorner Whimsey	65	90									
Spittoon Whimsey, very rare	1800										3200 LV
WREATH OF ROSES (FENTON)											
Bonbon	40	100	80	125							
Bonbon, stemmed	40	75	70	100					225		
Compote	45	55	50	50							
Punch Bowl w/base	400	575	700	900	2200						
Punch Bowl w/base, square top, very rare		2300									
Punch Cup	20	30	40	40	320						
WREATH OF ROSES VARIANT											
Compote	55	65	65	60							
ZIG ZAG (FENTON)											
Pitcher, decorated	425			450				600			
Tumbler, decorated	50			80				75			
ZIG ZAG (MILLERSBURG)											
Bowl, 5½" – 6½", ruffled, rare	500										
Bowl, square, 6", very rare	900										
Bowl, tricornered, 6½", very rare	900										
Bowl, round or ruffled, 9½"	125	225	325								
Bowl, 10", ice cream shape	400	550	1200								
Bowl, square, 8½" – 9½"	550	800	950								500 CM
Bowl, tricornered, 10"	500	750	900								
Card Tray, rare			1100								
ZIG ZAG (NORTHWOOD)											
Pitcher, very rare*		5000		800							
Tumbler, very rare*		500									
*(Experimental samples)											
ZIPPERED HEART (IMPERIAL)											
Bowl, 5"	40	65									
Bowl, 9"	85	110									
Queens Vase, rare	4200	4800	5500								
Rose Bowl, 5", very rare	1200										
Giant Rose Bowl, very rare			5000								
ZIPPER LOOP (IMPERIAL)											
Hand Lamp, two types, rare	825										1500 SM
Small Lamp, 7", rare	500										800 SM
Medium Lamp, 8", rare	550										600 SM
Large Lamp, 10", rare	450										500 SM
ZIPPER STITCH (CZECH)											
Bowl, 10", oval	125										
Cordial Set (tray, decanter, and four cordials), complete	1400										
ZIPPER VARIANT											
Bowl, oval, 10"	60										
Sugar w/lid	35										50 LV
ZIP ZIP (ENGLISH)											
Flower Frog Holder	60										